LUKE

JOHN

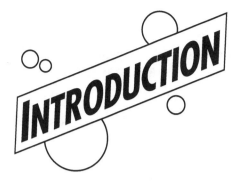

Quick Questions about *Quick Studies*

We've made *Quick Studies* as self-explanatory as possible, so you can dive in and start using them right away. But just in case you were wondering . . .

When should I use *Quick Studies*?

Whenever you want high school or junior high kids to explore the Bible face-to-face and absorb it into their lives. We've kept the openers active and the discussion questions creative, so you can use *Quick Studies* with confidence in Sunday school, midweek youth Bible study, small groups, even youth group meetings and retreats.

What's so quick about *Quick Studies*?

They're designed to save you preparation time. The session plans are compact, for quick reading. There aren't a lot of materials to gather, either (you'll need Bibles, pencils and paper, copies of the reproducible sheets, and sometimes a few other items). Yet *Quick Studies* are *real* Bible studies, with plenty of thought-provoking discussion and life application.

How are these different from other youth Bible studies?

We like to think *Quick Studies* are . . .

• *Irresistible.* You already know most kids don't jump at the chance to fill in a bunch of blanks in a boring study guide. So we used creative, reproducible sheets and *active* activities to draw kids into Scripture.

• *Involving.* You need discussion *starters*, not discussion *stoppers*. We avoided dull "yes or no" questions and included lots of thought-provokers that should get your group members talking about important issues. And we didn't forget suggested *answers* to most of the tougher questions, which should make things easier for you.

• *Inductive.* Many Bible studies try to force-feed kids a single "aim" and ignore other points Scripture is trying to make. *Quick Studies* let kids discover a variety of key principles in a passage.

• *Influential.* It's not enough to know what the Bible says. Every session includes a step designed to help kids decide what to do *personally* with vital points from the chapter.

When do kids read the passages covered?
That's up to you. If your group is into homework, assign the passages in advance. If not, take time to read the Scripture together after the "Opening Act" step that kicks off each session. There are dozens of ways to read a passage—with volunteers taking turns, or with a narrator and actors "performing" a scene, or with kids underlining points as they read silently, or with you reading as the author and kids listening as the original audience, or with small groups paraphrasing as they read . . .

What if I want to cover more—or less—than a chapter in a session?
Quick Studies is flexible. Each 45- to 60-minute session covers a chapter of the New Testament, but you can adjust the speed to fit your group. To cover more than one chapter in a session, just pick the points you want to emphasize and drop the activities, questions, and reproducible sheets you don't need. To cover less than a chapter, you may need to add a few questions and spend more time discussing the "So What?" application step in detail.

Do I have to cover a whole New Testament book?
No. Each session stands alone. Use sessions one at a time if you want to, or mix and match books in any order you choose. No matter how you use them, *Quick Studies* are likely to help your group see Bible study in a whole new light.

John Duckworth, Series Editor

LUKE 1

Guess Who's Having a Baby?

Luke begins his narrative on the life of Jesus with some events that took place before Jesus' birth: the angel Gabriel's visits to Zechariah and Mary, the miraculous pregnancy of Elizabeth, Mary's trip to see Elizabeth, and the birth of John the Baptist.

Hand out the reproducible sheet, "Christmas Presents," and have kids get into small groups. Once they've read the directions, give them time to silently decide which items they want in what order. Then have them compare within the groups and see how they made out for Christmas (no matter what time of year it is). Discuss: **Before this meeting, when was the last time you thought about Christmas? Have you thought much about what was going on nine months *before* the first Christmas? This chapter tells us about that.**

DATE I USED THIS SESSION _____ GROUP I USED IT WITH _____

NOTES FOR NEXT TIME_____

_____

_____

1. Luke wrote his Gospel to tell a friend about how special Jesus was (vss. 1-4). When was the last time you went out of your way to write or tell a friend about how special Jesus is to you? If you wrote down everything you know personally to be true about Jesus, how long would your "Gospel" be?

2. Many people at this time in history believed that a couple's inability to have children was a sign of God's disfavor. Zechariah and Elizabeth were unable to have children (vss. 5-7). **How do you think they felt?** (It was probably difficult for them to feel judged and misunderstood, just as it would be for us.)

3. Zechariah and Elizabeth continued to serve God faithfully, even though they didn't get what they wanted. **Does your obedience to God ever depend on what you receive from Him? How?** See if kids are willing to take whatever God provides. Or do some expect tangible benefits in return for their efforts? Do others try to get closer to God only when they want something special from Him?

4. Gabriel explained that God was going to give Zechariah and Elizabeth a wonderful gift—a son. If you were Zechariah, what questions would have run through your mind as the angel made his speech (vss. 13-17)? (Other than the one Zechariah asked in verse 18, he might have wondered what kind of son this would be, what incredible things he was going to do, whether he would somehow have to train the boy to do them, etc.)

5. The world would get plenty of benefits from Zechariah's son, but God had some expectations, too (vss. 8-17)—such as John's name and lifetime abstinence. **What do you think God expects from you if He gives you the following: (a) musical ability; (b) athletic talent; (c) an outgoing personality; (d) a comfortable home?**

6. God's command to Zechariah and Elizabeth was to do the thing they wanted so much—to have a baby (verses 18-25)! **Do you think God wants to fulfill the desires of your heart, or does He only want you to do things you'd hate? Why?**

7. Many scholars believe that Mary got Gabriel's incredible news when she was still a teenager. Suppose you (or your girlfriend) had received the message relayed in verses 26-37. How do you think you would respond? What do you think your parents would say? Your friends? (This news would obviously have a serious impact on their relationships with friends and family members. Their reputations would probably suffer.) Do you think the news was more embarrassing for Mary, or for Joseph? Why?

8. When something awesome happens in your life, who do you most want to tell? Is there any news you'd rather tell a Christian friend than a non-Christian one? Explain.

9. Since Mary and Elizabeth were both experiencing miraculous pregnancies, they decided to spend some time together (vss. 39-45, 56). What might we learn from this? (When God is doing wonderful things in our lives, we benefit by being around other believers with whom we can share our joy. Others can't fully understand.)

10. How do you think Zechariah felt after about a month of silence? After four months? After he was able to talk again (vss. 57-79)? If God made you unable to speak every time you doubted Him, would you have much to say? Since He doesn't do that, do you take advantage of the fact that you can freely express doubts to Him? If so, how? If not, why not?

(Needed: Guitar or other accompaniment [optional])

This chapter includes two songs—Mary's (vss. 46-55) and Zechariah's (vss. 68-79). Form two groups (girls in one and guys in another, if possible). Have each paraphrase one of the songs, to be sung to the tune of a hymn or chorus. Each team should add a second verse praising God for things He has done for members of the team. Then have the teams present their songs to the whole group.

CHRISTMAS PRESENTS

You have just been handed the following Christmas list. You may now silently choose 5 items you want next Christmas. However, you must rank the 5 items you choose in order of your most desired item (#1) to the least desired (#5). The catch is that if someone in your group chooses any of the same items as you, only one of you can get that item. Each item is one-of-a-kind. The one who gets the item is the one who has ranked it as the most desirable. If there is a tie, you must share the item. Have fun.

Brand-new, shiny, red sports car of your choice

A date with the movie star of your choice

An appearance on the talk show of your choice

An appearance in the next big science fiction movie

Season tickets to the pro football and baseball teams of your choice

Two months' vacation from school with no make-up work required

Big-screen TV and VCR with 25 free videos, entertainment system with 25 free CDs, and Super-Nintendo with 25 free games

Lifetime membership to the health club of your choice

All-expenses-paid trip for you and your family to Disney World

Six complete outfits from the clothing store of your choice

Lunch with the President of the United States

The ability to start a mission school named after you which will help educate 1,000 children in Haiti

A season's ski package at Aspen, Colorado, complete with condo at the foot of the slopes and unlimited airfare to get you back and forth on weekends

A million dollars donated in your name to further the environmental cause of your choice

Guaranteed acceptance to the college of your choice

LUKE 2

What Child Is This, Anyway?

CHAPTER ✓ CHECK

While Mary and Joseph are in Bethlehem for a census, the time comes for Jesus to be born. His birth is announced by angels and attended by shepherds. Eight days later, as Jesus is presented in the temple, He is praised by Simeon and Anna. Later, when Jesus is 12, His parents begin to see that His is to be no ordinary life.

OPENING ACT

(Needed: Colored paper, markers, other craft supplies)

Provide craft supplies for making greeting cards. Say: **If you had to design a greeting card that would tell people the real meaning of Christmas, what might it say? How might it look? Try making a card that does just that. The catch is that your card is to be sent in July, not December. And you can't use the word Christmas. And you can't show snow, trees, a manger scene, or Santa Claus. You've got five minutes!** Have kids work in small groups or individually. Then have them display and discuss the results. How did making the cards help them narrow down what the meaning of Christ's birth really is?

DATE I USED THIS SESSION _____ GROUP I USED IT WITH _____

NOTES FOR NEXT TIME _____

_____

_____

1. If Jesus were born in the U.S. or Canada today instead of 2,000 years ago in Bethlehem, how do you think this would happen? Where do you think He would be born, and to what kind of parents? (Point out that the birth of God's Son was not a big news event at the time. The parents were simple, humble people. And when the "invitations" went out, most of the recipients were on a lower rung of society's ladder. It might be the same today.)

2. To fulfill the prophecies concerning the Messiah (see Micah 5:2), **God used the mighty Roman Empire to get Mary and Joseph to the right place, Bethlehem** (vss. 1-5). **What powers in the world today do you think God might be working through to accomplish His plans?** (God can work through anything He wants to, including evil forces [Habakkuk 1:1-6] to carry out His plans.)

3. If God is powerful enough to control empires and allow virgins to give birth, couldn't He have come up with a motel room for Mary and Joseph (vss. 6, 7)? If so, why do you think He didn't? (Point out that even Jesus' birth shows the humility He would teach and model throughout life. From a human standpoint, Jesus had no advantages that we don't have—which makes us better able to follow His example for how to live.)

4. The shepherds responded right away to the angels' announcement (vss. 8-14). If they hadn't, do you think they would ever have known what they missed? How might their lives have been changed by this experience?

5. Have you ever gone a little bit out of your normal routine to find out more about Jesus? What happened? (Discuss how the results of even our small decisions may influence our spiritual development more than we know.)

6. Verse 27 says Simeon was "moved by the Spirit" and went into the temple courts. What do you think this means? Have you ever felt that God wanted you to do something specific? What happened as a result?

7. If you had prayed for ten years that God would send you a girlfriend or boyfriend and nothing had happened, how would you feel? What kept Simeon and Anna (vss. 25-38) going for much longer? (Endurance, patience, faithfulness over the long haul, etc.) How would you feel if that boyfriend or girlfriend finally showed up? How do you think Simeon and Anna felt when they finally saw the Messiah?

8. Mary had a habit of "treasuring things up in her heart" (vss. 19, 51). What kinds of things do you tend to store in your heart?

9. Jesus was misunderstood by His earthly parents (vs. 50), but He obeyed them (vs. 51). On a scale of 1 to 10 (10 highest), how hard would that be for you? (Point out that Jesus could have "pulled rank" on Mary and Joseph, but didn't. That doesn't leave us with many excuses for disobeying our parents.)

Hand out the student sheet, "Out of Whack," and have kids complete it. After they've had a chance to think about how they can grow in their weakest area, discuss. Some questions you might use: **If you really had wisdom, would you let any of the other three areas get out of balance? Would God "favor" anyone who didn't have wisdom? Is one of these areas more or less important than the others? How can this group help you grow in all four areas?**

OUT OF WHACK

"And Jesus grew in wisdom and stature, and in favor with God and men" (Luke 2:52).			
WISDOM ability to apply knowledge to make the right choices.	**STATURE** physical development.	**FAVOR WITH GOD** having a close, obedient relationship with Him.	**FAVOR WITH MEN** having a good reputation, relating well to people.

Jesus was a well-rounded person as He grew up. He developed in all four of these areas. But what happens when we get out of balance and develop in just one or two areas? Take a look at these.

LOTS OF WISDOM, BUT NO STATURE.

LOTS OF FAVOR WITH MEN (AND WOMEN), BUT NO FAVOR WITH GOD.

LOTS OF STATURE, BUT NO WISDOM.

LOTS OF FAVOR WITH GOD, BUT NO FAVOR WITH MEN (OR WOMEN).

How are you doing in keeping these four areas balanced?
Which are you strongest in? Weakest? Rank them from 1 (strongest) to 4 (weakest):

WISDOM	**STATURE**	**FAVOR WITH GOD**	**FAVOR WITH MEN**
What can you do in the next year to strengthen your weakest area?			

LUKE 3

Blazing a Trail

John the Baptist has begun to proclaim the coming of the Messiah. Preaching and baptizing in the desert, John calls people to repent and provides some guidelines on preparing for the kingdom of God. When Jesus comes to be baptized, it becomes obvious that He is someone special. (A genealogy is provided at this point in Luke's account to show exactly who Jesus is.)

Announce that you're going to have a special visitor today. Name the visitor (a celebrity of your choice, someone group members think is cool). The group's job is to prepare your meeting place for that person's appearance—in three minutes. See what kids do to prepare. Do they pick up trash from the floor—or make things messier? Do they try to make themselves look cool? After three minutes, announce that there's been a mistake; your visitor is actually someone else—someone who uses a wheelchair. The group has three minutes to make your room accessible. (If you have a group member who uses a wheelchair, make this visitor a two-year-old child and have the group childproof the room in three minutes.) Finally, announce that you were mistaken again—that the real visitor is Jesus Himself. See how kids react. Then discuss the mission of John the Baptist: to prepare the way for Jesus.

DATE I USED THIS SESSION _____ GROUP I USED IT WITH _____

NOTES FOR NEXT TIME _____

_____

_____

1. Do you have anything at home that's valuable, but doesn't necessarily look that way? (Examples: a coin, a baseball card, something of sentimental value.) **It takes an expert to tell the real value of some things. Jesus' value would be overlooked by a lot of people. If your job was to call attention to His value when He started His ministry, how would you have done it?**

2. Luke begins this chapter (vss. 1, 2) **by describing who was over the nation (Tiberius Caesar) and the religious community (Annas and Caiaphas). He ends it by showing who's really in charge (Jesus). Who are some people who expect you to be loyal to them? Does this ever interfere with your loyalty to Jesus? If so, how do you handle it?**

3. John began his ministry by "preaching a baptism of repentance for the forgiveness of sins" (vs. 3). **Why make a big deal about repentance? Why not just forgive everybody?** (Before Jesus forgives sins, we must first be aware of them, and then sorry about them. Repentance is a turning away from the wrong ways of doing things—a necessary first step.)

4. What do you think would be the title of John's sermon if he preached in our church today?

5. When was the last time you told someone that he or she needed to repent? Why? (Most kids probably have never done this. They may fear being misunderstood, turning people off, not being able to practice what they preach, etc.) **Do you think it was easy for John to tell people this? Why or why not?**

6. Do you think those crowds could understand what John wanted to get across to them (vss. 10-14)? (John's message was simple: Share with each other; be honest in business; tell the truth, etc.) **Do you feel you get such straight, practical answers to your questions about living the Christian life? What question could you use practical help with right now?** (Write these down to deal with in a future meeting.)

7. John was so popular that the people hoped he was their Messiah, but he directed their attention to Christ, who was yet to come. Who do you want to be more popular at your school—you or Jesus? How could you direct other kids' attention to Him?

8. Eventually John's direct approach to truth got him in trouble (vss. 19, 20). What would you have done in his place: been completely honest no matter what, or backed off a little because it was the leader of the land who was sinning? Why?

9. When Jesus was baptized (vss. 21, 22), what happened that proved the things John had taught about Him? Why was this important? (His special nature was confirmed by the other two members of the Trinity—God the Father, and the Holy Spirit. Anybody could claim to be God's Son, and there had been other "Messiah wannabes.")

10. People during this time thought Jesus was the son of Joseph, not the Son of God. What percentage of people in our country do you think believe that today? (Point out that verses 23-38 take Jesus' genealogy not just back to Adam, but to God.)

Hand out the student sheet, "A Kid Named John." After kids complete the sheet, discuss: **Did you feel embarrassed at the idea of John the Baptist participating in any of these activities? Why?** Encourage kids to go back through the list and reflect on how they think *Jesus* might want to participate with them in these activities in the future.

A KID NAMED JOHN

Circle the statements which you think best apply.

Suppose John the Baptist, as a teenager, attended your school.

What do you think he would look like?
- a "hunk" poster in *Tiger Beat* magazine
- pretty much like me
- a guy who just visited the Goodwill store
- something the cat dragged in
- other _____

How popular do you think he would be?
- big man on campus
- pretty much like me
- "Oh, no, here comes that weirdo again!"
- John who?
- other _____

Which of these activities would you like to do with him?

	Definitely!				No Way!
Double date	1	2	3	4	5
Go to dinner (girls)	1	2	3	4	5
Share a gym locker (guys)	1	2	3	4	5
Eat lunch in the cafeteria	1	2	3	4	5
Shop for clothes	1	2	3	4	5
Share the Gospel with your friends	1	2	3	4	5
Go to a horror movie	1	2	3	4	5
Play tackle football	1	2	3	4	5
Listen to your favorite radio station	1	2	3	4	5

LUKE 4

Tempt-a-thon

CHAPTER CHECK ✓

Preparing to begin His ministry, Jesus goes into the wilderness to be tempted by the devil. Soon after that He is rejected—and almost killed—by the people in His own hometown of Nazareth. Later He moves on, casting an evil spirit out of a man and healing others of all kinds of diseases.

OPENING ACT

Stage the following roleplay. Let one volunteer play himself on the Friday night before a big paper is due. He or she knows it will take every bit of the weekend to get it done. Then have other group members "call" or "drop by" as the person is trying to get the paper done. The other group members try to get the first student to go to the beach, to a movie, etc. See whether anyone can make an offer so tempting that the first student stops working. Then discuss the tempting tactics kids tried, and their similarity to those the devil uses on us. Point out that this chapter describes how Satan tried to sidetrack Jesus from His mission.

DATE I USED THIS SESSION _____ GROUP I USED IT WITH _____

NOTES FOR NEXT TIME _____

_____

_____

1. If the number of temptations you faced this month were "times at bat," the number of times you resisted were hits, and the number of times you gave in were outs, what do you think your batting average would be?

2. Why do you think people give in to temptations that they say they want to resist? (Some possibilities: They don't know how to wait patiently; selfish desires; not thinking through the possible consequences; spirit willing but flesh weak, etc.)

3. If Jesus was the perfect, sinless Son of God, how could He have been tempted (vss. 1, 2)? (In His humanity, He was subject to temptation. He had to choose whether or not to obey God's will, as we must. Also, His temptations allow Him now to know *exactly* how it feels to be tempted as we are.)

4. The first temptation dealt with His physical needs (vss. 3, 4). What do you think we can learn from the way Jesus fended off this attack? (Physical needs such as hunger are quick to capture our attention. But when they do, we need to remember that we were put on earth to do more than eat, drink, have sex, or whatever else the physical temptation might be.)

5. A second temptation was to Jesus' potential desire for power (vss. 5-8). What kinds of power could tempt a person your age? (Power to make your friends do what you want; power over the opposite sex; power to rebel against parents and do as you please; power in student government, etc.) How could you resist that kind of temptation? (By remembering that God is the only one with true power [vs. 8].)

6. A third temptation was to "put on a show," forcing God to act to protect Jesus (vss. 9-12). How do Christians today fall for that kind of temptation? (Some test God by claiming that He is obligated to keep them healthy and wealthy. Some believe that handling snakes are "faith acts" which demand God's protection. God honors faith based on the whole counsel of Scripture, not silly or selfish demands based on misapplied portions of Scripture that conveniently fit our wishes.) **Is it ever good to take risks and count on God to rescue you? If so, when?**

7. **When do you think you'll stop being tempted** (vs. 13)? (Not in this life. The tempter is waiting for "an opportune time." In fact, sometimes, the stronger our faith becomes, the more deceptive the temptations get.) **How do you feel about that?**

8. **What were some of the things Jesus accomplished for the people who had faith in Him** (vss. 31-41)? **What does that mean to you today?** (Faith in Jesus led to the casting out of evil spirits, healing from fever, and healing for "various kinds of sickness." Jesus is no less powerful today. We need to not only take our physical and spiritual concerns to Him, but also have faith that He can help us.)

9. **In the midst of his busyness, Jesus made time to be alone with His Father** (vss. 42-44). **Why?** (As popular and powerful as He was, Jesus knew He needed to maintain His personal relationship with the Father. He knew that activity "for God" can never replace intimacy with God.) **If you could spend a "perfect" 15 minutes with God, what would it be like?**

Hand out the student sheet, "Luring Lines." Give kids a chance to complete the sheet; then discuss their answers as much as they're willing. Ask : **Have you ever thought about the fact that Jesus was once a teenager like you? What difference does that make?** Have someone read Hebrews 2:18 and then Hebrews 4:15, 16. Encourage kids to go back to their "Temptometers" and pick out one area where they're "sweating bullets." Encourage them to talk to Jesus about that area, since they can be confident that His understanding, and help are just a prayer away.

Luring Lines

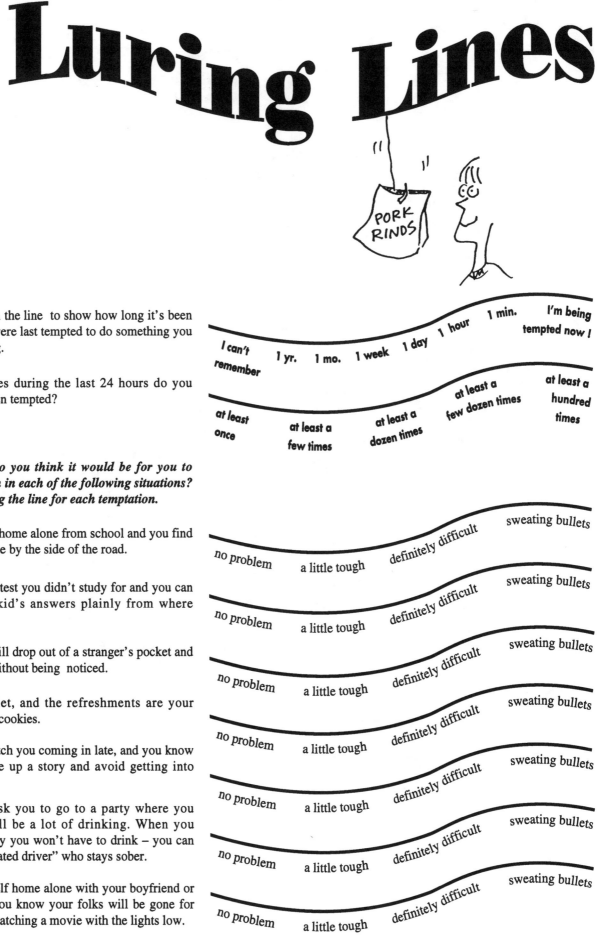

Mark an X on the line to show how long it's been since you were last tempted to do something you knew was wrong.

How many times during the last 24 hours do you think you've been tempted?

I can't remember   1 yr.   1 mo.   1 week   1 day   1 hour   1 min.   I'm being tempted now !

at least once   at least a few times   at least a dozen times   at least a few dozen times   at least a hundred times

How difficult do you think it would be for you to resist temptation in each of the following situations? Mark an X along the line for each temptation.

You're walking home alone from school and you find a porno magazine by the side of the road.

no problem   a little tough   definitely difficult   sweating bullets

You're taking a test you didn't study for and you can see the smart kid's answers plainly from where you're sitting.

no problem   a little tough   definitely difficult   sweating bullets

You see a $20 bill drop out of a stranger's pocket and you pick it up without being noticed.

no problem   a little tough   definitely difficult   sweating bullets

You're on a diet, and the refreshments are your favorite kind of cookies.

no problem   a little tough   definitely difficult   sweating bullets

Your parents catch you coming in late, and you know you could make up a story and avoid getting into trouble.

no problem   a little tough   definitely difficult   sweating bullets

Your friends ask you to go to a party where you know there will be a lot of drinking. When you hesitate, they say you won't have to drink – you can be their "designated driver" who stays sober.

no problem   a little tough   definitely difficult   sweating bullets

You find yourself home alone with your boyfriend or girlfriend and you know your folks will be gone for hours. You're watching a movie with the lights low.

no problem   a little tough   definitely difficult   sweating bullets

LUKE 5

The Call

As Jesus becomes more of a public figure, He begins to select disciples. He continues to teach, this time about fasting. He also explains the connection between His ability to heal people and His right to forgive sins. And He is criticized by the Pharisees for His choice of friends.

(Needed: Prize [optional])

Ask for three volunteers. Explain that each is going to become a "social outcast" for the next few minutes. The reason: Each has a big glob of something stuck to him or her. Have one volunteer leave the room. While the person is gone, the rest of the group should decide what kind of glob it is and where it's stuck (for example, a glob of pond scum on his or her nose). When the volunteer returns, he or she can ask up to 20 yes-or-no questions to try to find out the what and where of the glob. Do the same with the other two volunteers. The winner is the one (if any) who identifies the nature and location of the glob in the fewest questions. Then ask how the "social outcasts" felt. Point out that Jesus was criticized in this chapter for befriending "outcasts."

DATE I USED THIS SESSION _____ GROUP I USED IT WITH _____

NOTES FOR NEXT TIME _____

_____

_____

1. What's the worst advice you've ever gotten? The best advice? (After kids respond, call attention to Jesus' advice in vs. 4.)

2. If you'd been in Peter's position, what do you think you would have done in response to Jesus' advice (vs. 4)? (An experienced fisherman might not heed the fishing advice of a carpenter. And most people don't respond too well to requests at the end of a long workday [or night] when they're tired and cranky.)

3. What do you think Peter was risking by doing what Jesus asked? (People laughing at him if he caught nothing; not getting home at a decent hour, etc.) Do you think the result was worth the risk (vss. 5-7)? What's the riskiest thing you could do for Jesus this week? What do you think would happen if you did it? (Anytime we put Jesus first, we're likely to be surprised [or downright shocked] at the results.)

4. Why did Jesus' "fishing skill" make Peter worry about his own sin (vss. 8-10)? (He knew Jesus must have been sent from God.) When do you tend to be most aware of your sins: (a) during Communion; (b) while you're sinning; (c) only if you get caught; (d) when you pray; (e) some other time? Why?

5. The day Peter stopped being a catcher of fish for a living, he became a catcher of people instead (vss. 10, 11). What changes have you experienced since the day you said good-bye to your "old" life and began following Jesus?

6. How are you like the leper (vss. 12-14) when it comes to asking the Lord for something? How are you different? (Examples: I'm reluctant to ask for things, feeling God might not be willing to help me; I tend to ask casually instead of begging, etc.)

7. Look at the story of the paralyzed man and his friends (vss. 17-26). How easy is it for disabled people to get into our church? Our group? What barriers might our attitudes create for *any* kids who would like to get closer to Jesus?

8. After Jesus called Levi (Matthew) to be a disciple, Levi threw a party for Jesus and invited lots of his friends (vss. 27-32). The Pharisees frowned on it, but Jesus defended His involvement with "sinners." In what ways are you trying to connect your non-Christian friends with Jesus? How could you do more of that?

9. What do you think Jesus is getting at in vss. 33-39? (The teachings of Jesus are so new and unique that no one else's can compare. Some will try to "bottle up" Jesus' new way in old structures and entangle it with man-made rules, but that won't work.)

10. Has Christianity been around for so long that it seems like "old stuff" to you? What is the "new" part of the Good News? (The Gospel is always new to those who haven't heard it—or those who have heard but haven't understood it. And the everyday effect Jesus has on our lives should always be new.)

Hand out the reproducible sheet, "Under the Sea." This sheet illustrates Jesus' call to His followers to ever-increasing depths of intimacy with and commitment to Him. When kids finish, discuss the results if they're willing. Especially note the ways in which some, if any, would like to go deeper and learn more. How can you respond as you plan future topics and activities for your group?

UNDER THE SEA

PUDDLE DEPTH

POND DEPTH

PACIFIC DEPTH

One day Jesus told Peter to, "Put out into deep water, and let down the nets for a catch" (Luke 5:4). When Peter reluctantly obeyed, things started to happen. The nets began to break, so Peter's fellow fishermen called for help. The overflow of fish was so great that both boats began to sink. In the midst of this whirlwind of activity, Peter recognized his own sinfulness and the greatness of the One standing before Him. That very day he left everything else behind and followed Jesus.

What do you think would happen if you began to "fish a little deeper"? In this picture, extend the fishing line to illustrate the depth at which you feel you're "fishing" spiritually these days. At that level, write (on and around the fish) some of the things you feel you're learning about Jesus. Above that level, write some things you feel you've already learned. And below that level, record some things you would still like to learn about Jesus or accomplish for Him.

LUKE 6

Faith of the Living Dead

As word about Jesus continues to spread, He attracts large crowds seeking healing, and He has some inevitable conflicts with the Pharisees. He also selects twelve of His followers to serve as apostles and begins to teach them how God's people should live their lives.

(Needed: Prize [optional])

Have kids complete the reproducible sheet, "Oh, the Pain!" Then tally the results (adding up the total time in the left-hand column on each sheet). If you like, award an "Iron Man (or Woman)" prize to the person who claimed he or she could endure the most pain. Ask: **When have you voluntarily endured pain?** (Going to the dentist; football camp; trying to impress someone else, etc.) **We can put up with almost anything if we know it's not going to last forever. That's what Jesus asks of us in this chapter—to put up with discomfort and injustice now, knowing that God will someday put an end to it and provide us with something far better.**

DATE I USED THIS SESSION _____ GROUP I USED IT WITH _____

NOTES FOR NEXT TIME _____

_____

_____

1. What are your favorite things to do on Saturday afternoon? On a Sunday afternoon?

2. For what two Sabbath activities did Jesus receive criticism (vss. 1-11)? (Allowing His disciples to pick grain, and healing other people.) **What was His defense?** (It's never the wrong time to do good for others; He is "Lord of the Sabbath." The problem was with the Pharisees' short-sighted application of the Sabbath law—not with the law itself.)

3. What was the last major decision you had to make? What process do you go through to help you make important decisions?

4. What do verses 12-16 tell you about how Jesus made important decisions? (He spent a whole night in prayer before choosing the 12. He really must have wanted to do His Father's will.)

5. Much of the time Jesus was surrounded by diseased, possessed, and otherwise troubled people (vss. 17-19). He healed many, but also taught that life wouldn't always go smoothly. What were some of the things He said the people of God could expect (vss. 20-26)? (Poverty, hunger, weeping, rejection, and persecution.) **Which of these do you think God might allow you to suffer? What might be your reaction if He did?**

6. Can you remember the last time you had a chance to love your enemies (vss. 27-36)? How did it turn out? Why do you think Jesus wants us to love our enemies, anyway? (The ability to love those who don't show love for us reflects the nature of God and sets us apart from the rest of the world.)

7. When's the last time you really felt judged by someone? Why do you think Jesus is not big on us judging each other (vss. 37-42)? (Nobody but God is sinless, so we all need a healthy dose of mercy and forgiveness. Nobody needs another critic.)

8. If your thoughts and attitudes actually were turned into fruit (vss. 43-45), what do you think it would look like? How would it taste? Why?

9. Look at verse 46. If you had to wear to school a big pin that said, "Jesus Is Lord," how might your behavior change? What might be a better way to show that Jesus is Lord of your life?

10. How is the story of the builders (vss. 47-49) like the story of the "Three Little Pigs"? What kinds of storms have tested the strength of your foundation?

Say: **For each of the following situations, tell what you'd do if you were just concerned about your own short-term comfort. Then explain how you might respond if you were willing to sacrifice your own desires and feelings—just for now—for Jesus' sake.**

• **You and another person are being considered for a key position (cheerleader, first chair clarinet, etc.). The other person wins, but then you find out (s)he cheated. You have hard evidence to prove it.**

• **A person at school who makes fun of you gets mono and can't come to classes for several weeks. When the teacher looks for someone to carry assignments back and forth, no one volunteers. This person lives fairly close to you, but the job would mean seeing him or her every day during your only period of free time.**

• **You finally save up enough to buy a car. The first day you drive it to school, your little brother decides to invite all his friends to eat lunch in it—and they get melted cheese all over the seats.**

OH, THE *PAIN!*

How tough are you? For each painful experience below, write in how long you think you could endure it before screaming, crying, or passing out.

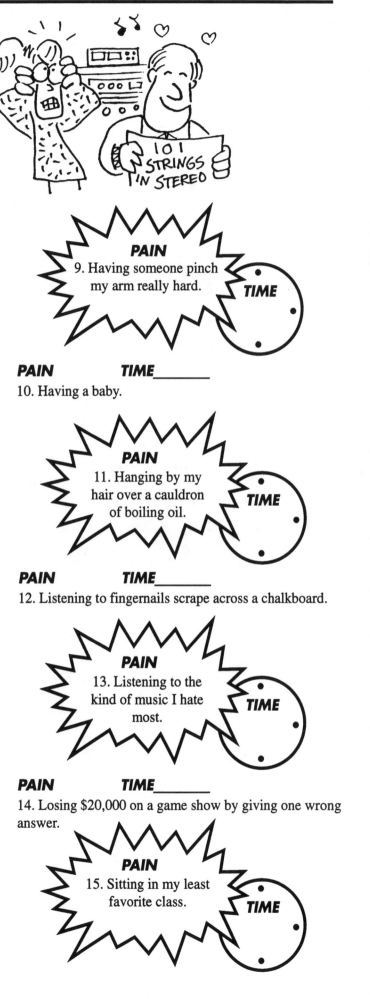

PAIN   **TIME**_____

1. Having someone pound on my thumb with a hammer.

PAIN
2. Having someone pound on my ankle with a sledgehammer.   **TIME**

PAIN   **TIME**_____

3. Lying on a bed of nails.

PAIN
4. Walking barefooted across burning coals.   **TIME**

PAIN   **TIME**_____

5. Letting my youth leader stand on my foot.

PAIN
6. Holding my hand two inches above a candle flame.   **TIME**

PAIN   **TIME**_____

7. Hiking with a sharp rock in my shoe.

PAIN
8. Being totally alone, rejected by everyone.   **TIME**

PAIN
9. Having someone pinch my arm really hard.   **TIME**

PAIN   **TIME**_____

10. Having a baby.

PAIN
11. Hanging by my hair over a cauldron of boiling oil.   **TIME**

PAIN   **TIME**_____

12. Listening to fingernails scrape across a chalkboard.

PAIN
13. Listening to the kind of music I hate most.   **TIME**

PAIN   **TIME**_____

14. Losing $20,000 on a game show by giving one wrong answer.

PAIN
15. Sitting in my least favorite class.   **TIME**

LUKE 7

Long-Distance Service

Jesus demonstrates that no problem is beyond the power of God as He first completes a "long-distance" healing of a centurion's servant, then raises a widow's son from the dead. Later He has a discussion with the disciples of John the Baptist, after which He commends John to the people around Him. Finally, He is anointed by a woman, which raises some eyebrows, but He explains her motives to those who question the act.

(Needed: Tissues and prize [optional])

Have a "Sob Story" contest. Each competitor should take up to a minute to explain to the rest of the group why his or her week was worse than anyone else's. The goal is to evoke all the pity possible. Pass out tissues to other group members and encourage them to wail and moan. When all volunteers have presented their sob stories, let the group vote for the "winner." Award a prize if you like. Ask: **When is crying good? When is it not? How do you feel when you're around someone who's crying?** Refer to this later when you discuss question #4.

DATE I USED THIS SESSION _____ GROUP I USED IT WITH _____

NOTES FOR NEXT TIME _____

_____

_____

1. Have you ever used a fax machine, computer, next-day delivery, credit cards, or a microwave oven? Do you think these are improvements over the older, slower ways of doing things? Why or why not? (Discuss both the pros, like no waiting—and cons, like people having less patience.)

2. Nearly 2,000 years before these things were dreamed of, a centurion in Capernaum believed Jesus was capable of instant, long-distance service. He wasn't even a Jewish person, yet his faith was great. Why do you think it impressed Jesus (vss. 1-10)? (The centurion believed Jesus could heal his servant with a command, without going Himself. That kind of faith really honors Jesus. We could use it today.)

3. In one of the next towns Jesus visited, Jesus came upon a funeral procession. What do you think you would have felt if you were one of the people carrying the boy's coffin (vss. 11-17)?

4. In Luke 6:21, Jesus says, "Blessed are you who weep." But to the mourning widow He says, "Don't cry" (7:13). Isn't this a contradiction? (Not really. The benefit of weeping is being comforted by God so that we can laugh again. Jesus was about to bring joy to the widow by raising her son. Point out that even though hard times are part of life and God can make them work for good, He doesn't enjoy seeing us suffer.)

5. What does Jesus' treatment of this woman and her son (vss. 11-17) **tell you about Him?** (His power is unlimited; He cares about the everyday pains of our lives, not just our souls after death; He doesn't always wait till we come begging to Him to act on our behalf, etc.)

6. John the Baptist, while in prison, sent messengers to make sure Jesus was really the Christ (vss. 18-23). Jesus said in effect, "Just go tell him what you see." If someone wanted to know if you were really a Christian, what do you think he or she would look for?

7. Not even Jesus could please everybody (vss. 29-35). Have you ever been criticized for being too serious, or too "Christian"? Has anyone given you a hard time for not being serious (or "Christian") enough? How can you tell whether you've got the right balance in this area? (Examples: Can you weep with those who weep and celebrate with those who are joyful? Are you "fun" enough to attract people to Jesus, but "serious" enough to help them receive Him?)

8. Why was Jesus so impressed with the actions of the woman described in verses 36-50? (Maybe because she knew she was a "big-time" sinner and worshiped in a "big-time" way.)

9. What do you think about people who don't worship Jesus the same way you do? What do you think Jesus thinks about them? (If the worship is genuine, He's honored by a child saying "God is great, God is good," an actor in a Passion Play, or any number of other methods—traditional and nontraditional.)

10. In what ways are you a little like Simon the Pharisee? How are you a little like the woman who anointed Jesus? How do you think Simon reacted after the events of this chapter?

Have kids work in small groups on the reproducible sheet, "Big Kids Don't Cry?" Various answers are possible. Let kids use all the verses and biblical principles they can think of. Stress that Jesus understands our suffering, and that He wants to change our tears to joy—though that may not happen for some time. If we let Him, He will be with us during the grieving process. Watch for hurts kids may be feeling now, and gather group support and affirmation for these kids if possible.

BIG kids don't CRY?

Grandparents die. Parents get divorced. Friends move away–or worse, they desert you for new friends and leave you feeling lost and alone.

Being a Christian is no vaccine from having any of these things happen to you. And many times crying is exactly the right thing to do–for guys as well as girls. But events like these don't have to crush you permanently. If you run to Jesus, He can see you through anything that comes your way.

That's hard to remember when things get tough. So . . .

In the left column below, you'll find some things that might make you want to cry, grieve, give up, get mad, quit, complain, or just zone out in your room and eat Twinkies all day. In the right column, write some reasons for hope, joy, faith, and just plain staying at it. For help, use any or all of the Bible passages listed at the bottom of the page.

Reasons to Cry	Reasons to Hope

1. It's the start of your senior year. You just found out that you have to move 2,000 miles away, where you won't know anyone but your parents and your dog.

2. You discover that a friend got the HIV virus that causes AIDS from a blood transfusion she had during an operation last year.

3. Summer vacation has started, but you can't find a job. If you can't make some money, you won't be able to start college next fall.

4. At a concert, somebody steals your wallet. You don't even have enough money to call home.

5. Your father hasn't been acting like himself lately. He refuses to talk to anyone for days at a time. Your mother keeps taking him to the doctor. Now she tells you that he will have to go to a mental hospital–for how long, nobody knows.

6. You're on a plane with other band members, coming back from a contest. There is an explosion in one of the engines, and the pilot announces that the plane will have to make an emergency landing–in the water.

7. Last night you saw a video at church about really getting serious with God. Now all you can think of is how you keep promising God that you won't think about sex so much, that you'll stop fantasizing. But you can't seem to stop. You feel out of control, guilty, worthless. You'll never be a "real" Christian like the kids in the video.

Promises and Other Passages

Exodus 33:14, Revelation 7:16, 17, Jude 24, 25, I Peter 1:6, 7; 5:7, Matthew 6:25-34, Philippians 4:6, 7, I John 1:9, II Corinthians 1:3, 4, Nehemiah 1:5, Psalm 23:4, Psalm 103:1-3, Psalm 119:105, Psalm 121:1, 2, Proverbs 3:5, 6, Psalm 71:14-16, Romans 8:38, 39, Zephaniah 3:17, Lamentations 3:22-24, Jeremiah 29:11; 32:17; 33:3, Isaiah 40:31; 43:1-3

Have You Got Ears?

Jesus challenges His listeners with the Parable of the Sower and the illustration of the lamp on a stand. He also quiets a storm, casts out evil spirits from a man, heals a woman with a long-term bleeding problem, and raises Jairus's daughter from the dead.

Read each of the following quotes. Have kids stand on one side of the room if they agree, another if they disagree. Ask volunteers to explain their "stands." **"Life is like licking honey off a thorn." "Life is like a game of cards: you can't control the cards you're dealt, but you can control how well you play them." "Life is what happens to us while we're making other plans." "Life is like learning to play the violin at your recital." "Life is a comedy to those who think, and a tragedy to those who feel."** Explain that these comparisons, like Jesus' parables in this chapter, are meant to make us stop and think hard about life.

DATE I USED THIS SESSION _____ GROUP I USED IT WITH _____

NOTES FOR NEXT TIME _____

_____

_____

1. What was your best success—or worst disaster—in trying to grow something?

2. Jesus seemed to "sow" at every opportunity. But how was His ministry being financed as He went from town to town (vss. 1-3)? (His faithful followers—many of them women—helped support Him.) **How could you support a ministry that you really believed in?** (Time, money, talents, etc.) **Can you name a ministry you think is worth supporting?**

3. Can you think of people you know who seem to fit each kind of soil Jesus describes (vss 4-15)? Which do you think describes you? (Let students respond and compare their answers to Jesus' explanations of each.)

4. How could you be like a "lamp on a stand" (vss. 16-18) in your home? At school? (Jesus is talking about explaining the meaning of His parables, so this could mean helping others to understand His teachings—especially the good news of salvation.)

5. Based on Jesus' definition in verse 21, how closely "related" to Him are most of the people in your school? How about you?

Read about Jesus' calming of the storm (vss. 22-25). Before discussing it, have four kids act out the skit on the reproducible sheet, "What If . . . ?" Introduce it by asking: **What if things had gone a little differently in the boat that day?** After having fun with the skit, ask: **How are we like the disciples in this skit when it comes to asking the Lord for help?** (We try to do things ourselves; we don't want to "bother" Him; we think He wouldn't know how to solve the problem, or that He would criticize us, etc.)

6. If you had been in the boat with the disciples (vss. 22-25), how do you think you would have responded to the storm? What's the first thing you would have done when the storm stopped?

7. When Jesus questioned the faith of His disciples, what do you think He meant? Do you think it's possible to have faith and feel afraid at the same time? How? (Fear is a natural response to danger. The issue is, how do we handle the fear? If God is really in control of nature and of our lives, we can act by faith in spite of our fear.)

8. Why do you think Jesus told the man He cast the demons out of to return home instead of following Him (vss. 26-39)? (Jesus was no longer welcome there. This man would be His living testimony to those who knew him before.) **How do you think people treated the man when he returned?**

9. After all Jesus had been trying to teach the disciples about faith, what do you think they learned from His raising of Jairus's young daughter (vss. 40-42, 49-56) **and His healing of the woman with the 12-year bleeding problem** (vss. 43-48)? (Perhaps that no problem is too much for Jesus to handle. Jesus healed both people, and faith was a key element.)

10. Let's say you could spend 15 minutes with anyone mentioned in this chapter—except Jesus. Your goal would be to increase your faith. Which person would you choose, and why?

Jesus told the formerly demon-possessed man to return home. It might have been fun and exciting to follow Jesus close-up, but the man had to tough it out at home. **What are some problems you face at home that make it hard for you to live out the things we talk about in this group?** Have kids share as a whole group or in small groups. Spend some time praying for each other's home lives. Try to follow up personally on any serious problems that are mentioned.

 What If...?

Characters: Disciple A, Disciple B, Disciple C, Disciple D
Setting: In a boat on the water; Jesus (unseen) is asleep in the back of the boat.

A: Hey, nice day for a sail, huh?

B: I thought we'd never get away from that crowd. Let's just relax.

C: The Teacher has the right idea. He's asleep.

D: Wait a minute. Where did those clouds come from?

A: I can't believe it! There's a storm coming up!

B: You said it was supposed to be sunny today!

C: Don't blame me! It was that stupid weatherman!

D: Man, what a wind! We're going to go under for sure!

A: Let's throw somebody overboard. It worked for Jonah.

B: No, that was in the Old Testament. This is different.

C: Maybe the Teacher will know what to do.

D: He was a carpenter, not a sailor.

A: No offense.

B: Besides, He's had a hard day. Let Him sleep.

C: But you saw what He can do with nature –
all those sick people, all that bread and fish . . .

D: But maybe He's not good with weather.

A: And if we wake Him up, He'll just tell us
we should have had more faith.

B: I'm not feeling well. I think I'm going to –

C: Hey, you'd better not throw up on me!

D: You're sick? Hey, guys, let's wake the
Teacher! He's great with illness!

All: Master, Master! HELP!!!

On-the-Job Training: Phase 1

CHAPTER CHECK

Jesus gives power to the twelve apostles and sends them out on some "short-term missions" projects. Later He tries to get them to feed a crowd of more than 5,000, but has to do it Himself. Peter makes a bold confession of who Jesus is, which is later verified as three of the disciples see Jesus' transfiguration. Jesus continues to heal, to teach the disciples, and to handle rejection.

OPENING ACT

Arrange before the meeting for one or two of your group members to burst into the group with masks or bandanas over their faces and carrying "loaded" squirt guns. Have the bandit(s) then go around the group demanding one item from each person. ("Victims" can simply lay the item on the floor in front of them.) After receiving one item per person, the bandit(s) are sent around again . . . and again. Anyone who puts up a fuss or fails to comply gets "shot." Observe how much kids give up before they start to complain. Note how many nonessential items they carry with them, and which items seem hardest to part with. Refer to this as you discuss the first part of this chapter.

DATE I USED THIS SESSION _____ GROUP I USED IT WITH _____

NOTES FOR NEXT TIME _____

_____

_____

1. Have you ever tried to buy something, but realized too late that you didn't have any—or enough—money? How did you feel?

2. When Jesus gave power to His disciples, why do you think He told them to travel light (vss. 1-6)? (God wants us to trust Him to be the source of our provision as well as our power. The more we depend on ourselves and our possessions, the less we depend on Him.)

3. When the disciples returned from their individual assignments, Jesus gave them two group projects that they couldn't complete (vss. 10-17 and 37-43). **Why do you think they failed?** (Possibilities: Lack of faith; they hadn't seen it done before; they focused more on the problems than on God's abilities, etc.)

4. Have you ever seen God stretch "a little" into "a lot"? (Examples: Money; food; at Hanukkah Jewish people celebrate a near-empty oil lamp miraculously burning for days, etc.) **What do you have a little of that you'd like God to stretch into a lot? What would you do with that "lot" if you had it?**

5. If someone asked you, "Who do you think Jesus really is, and what difference has He made in your life?" what would you say? (Compare with Peter's answer in verses 18-22.)

6. In verse 22 Jesus lays out what will happen to Him— His death and resurrection. How could the disciples have been surprised when these things happened later? (Maybe they weren't paying attention; maybe they thought it was another of Jesus' symbolic parables, etc.) **Have you ever prayed for something to happen—and it did? Were you surprised? Why?**

7. Do you think Jesus expects too much of His followers (vss. 23-27)? **Explain.** (Jesus does expect a lot—self-denial, taking up a cross and following Him, etc. But it's no more than He did for us. And He gives us the power to do these things if we ask.)

8. If you had been at the Transfiguration (vss. 28-36), what might you tell your grandchildren about it someday?

9. Right after the disciples failed to drive out an evil spirit (vss. 37-45), **they argued about who was the greatest** (vss. 46-50). **Shouldn't they have been too embarrassed to argue about that?** (Probably, but maybe they were boasting to make up for their feelings of failure.) **How do you tend to act after you've failed at something? Do you think God approves of that reaction?**

10. Do you think James and John could have destroyed the Samaritan village (vss. 51-56)? (Probably not, since Jesus was opposed to it and they'd already shown that their powers were pretty limited.) **Have you ever had the urge to "defend" God? What happened?**

11. Do you think Jesus was a little too hard on the people who wanted to follow Him, but who also wanted to care for their families, etc. (vss. 57-62)? (These are extreme statements, but they show that we should allow nothing to stand between ourselves and Jesus. Once we begin to justify our actions with excuses, it's hard to stop.)

Kids can consider the excuses they give for not wholeheartedly following Jesus as they fill out the student sheet, "But First . . ." Discuss the results if they're willing, but don't press. Ask: **Could any of these things be resolved if Jesus were helping you with them? Do you think a life committed to Jesus might eliminate some of these problems? How long do you expect Jesus to wait before you're willing to serve Him completely?** Encourage kids to ask God to help them evaluate these excuses, and to help them live an excuse-free life during the coming week.

BUT FIRST...

You've been around long enough to come up with excuses at a moment's notice. If your parents want you to do chores, you might say, "Hey, I have homework. You told me I had to get my grades up, right?" When the phone rings a few minutes later and someone from church needs your help, you might say, "Sorry. My folks have some chores they want me to do."

When it comes to following Jesus, He can see through all the mental gymnastics. He won't force us to follow Him. But we need to be honest with Him. So let's be honest right now.

Knowing that Jesus wants you to follow Him, to put Him first in every area of your life, what would you like to say to Him? Check any answer that applies to you; then write as many of your own responses as you feel necessary. It's time to be brutally honest.

Jesus, I want to follow You, but it's really hard. I would be a lot more ready to commit my whole life to You if only I could first . . .

____ know exactly what You'll ask of me down the road.

____ make a lot of money.

____ reach age 21.

____ get my career going.

____ get all my questions about the Bible answered.

____ get a "sign" from You, proving that You're there.

____ get the right boyfriend/girlfriend.

____ get in with the right crowd.

____ get better grades in school.

____ stop having problems at home with my family.

____ have at least a couple of really great friends.

____ have all the fun and excitement I can.

____ make the _____ team.

____ quit that one nasty habit that You and I both know about.

____ _____

____ _____

____ _____

____ _____

LUKE 10

On-the-Job Training: Phase 2

Jesus sends out 72 of His followers in pairs ahead of Him with specific instructions about what to say and how to behave. It's an exciting, eye-opening experience for them. Then, as Jesus teaches about love, He tells the Parable of the Good Samaritan. Later, at the home of Mary and Martha, He helps them establish the right priorities.

OPENING ACT

Hand out the reproducible sheet, "Stereotypewriter," and say: **Look at each of the following phrases and write down the first thing that comes to your mind for each. Be honest! No one else will see your papers. If you don't know what one means, or if nothing comes to mind, just move on.** Once everyone gets through the list (or after five minutes) ask kids to add up the number or complimentary, positive things they wrote—and then the number of not-so-complimentary, more negative things they wrote. Then go around the room and ask for their results: positive vs. negative. Don't be surprised if most have more negative than positive. You may want to refer to this when you discuss "the Good Samaritan."

DATE I USED THIS SESSION _____ GROUP I USED IT WITH _____

NOTES FOR NEXT TIME _____

_____

_____

1. What kind of group project would get you really excited?

2. When it comes to spreading the word about Jesus, would you rather be part of a big group, on a small team, or on your own? Why?

3. Why do you think Jesus sent the 72 out in pairs? (See Ecclesiastes 4:9-12.)

4. Do you think you would have wanted to be one of the 72 who were sent out? Why or why not?

5. If you were sending these messengers out, what kind of pep talk would you give them first? (Compare this with what Jesus said. He made it clear that this was not going to be fun and games. It would mean living simply, possibly facing hostility, danger, etc.) **Before you became a Christian (if you are), did anybody give you a "pep talk" about how great the Christian life would be? If so, do you feel let down now? If no one did, do you think someone should have? Why?**

6. If you were to write down everything it means to love God with all your heart, soul, strength and mind and your neighbor as yourself (vss. 25-28), how long do you think it would take? Can you sum up in 10 words or less what it means to you?

7. Look at verse 29. Has your idea of who your "neighbor" is shrunk as you've grown, or has it gotten wider? Do you care about more people's needs than you did a few years ago, or fewer people's needs?

8. Why, when Jesus knew that Jews hated Samaritans, do you think He chose one to be the hero of His story? Why did He choose a priest and a Levite to be "bad guys?"
(Jesus wanted to smash some stereotypes along with the false sense of superiority people feel when they use them.)

9. Why might God care about the way we stereotype people who are different from ourselves? (Stereotypes can make us care less about individuals and what happens to them; stereotyping others can be a sign of pride or even hate, etc.)

10. **Who are some "neighbors" that Jesus might be calling you to love?** (Outcasts at school; family members we fight a lot with; older relatives we've ignored, etc.)

11. **Why do you think Jesus came down so hard on Martha** (vss. 38-42)**? Wasn't she right, with a guest in the house, to try to make dinner, set the table, and be a proper hostess?** (Jesus emphasized many times that activities, no matter how religious or proper, are never an adequate substitute for a relationship with Him. When Jesus wants to communicate with us, nothing else should be more important, no matter how worthy the cause.)

(Needed: Chalkboard and chalk or newsprint and marker)

As a group, brainstorm activities your kids are involved in. As each activity is mentioned, try to decide as a group whether you think it should qualify as a "Martha-type activity" (busy, but not advancing our relationship with God) or a "Mary-type activity" (bringing us closer to God). Write each activity under the appropriate column heading (Martha or Mary) on a chalkboard or piece of newsprint. Then have each student look at the two lists and decide whether he or she is more like Mary or more like Martha. Finally, have each person pick one activity from each column—a "Martha" activity to do less, and a "Mary" activity to do more often.

stereoTYPEwriter

HOMELESS PERSON	POLITICIAN
WEALTHY PERSON	FOOTBALL PLAYER
POLISH PERSON	CHEERLEADER
FEMINIST	TELEVANGELIST
JEWISH PERSON	CONSTRUCTION WORKER
SCHOOL VICE-PRINCIPAL	HOMEMAKER
MARCHING BAND MEMBER	HISPANIC PERSON
GREENPEACE ACTIVIST	NUN
LAWYER	SORORITY MEMBER
ACCOUNTANT	FRATERNITY MEMBER
CANADIAN	JAPANESE PERSON
NATIVE AMERICAN	TRUCK DRIVER
AMERICAN WHITE PERSON	CULT MEMBER
AMERICAN BLACK PERSON	EX-CONVICT
AFRICAN BLACK PERSON	USED CAR SALESPERSON
BLONDE FEMALE	ATHEIST
COMMUNIST	ITALIAN PERSON
JAMAICAN PERSON	YOUTH PASTOR
ARAB MUSLIM	UNION OFFICIAL
IRISH CATHOLIC	APPALACHIAN PERSON

OVERMETAL

LUKE 11

A Model and A Menace

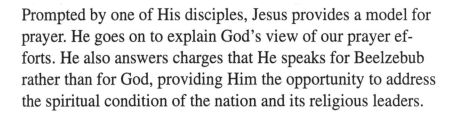

Prompted by one of His disciples, Jesus provides a model for prayer. He goes on to explain God's view of our prayer efforts. He also answers charges that He speaks for Beelzebub rather than for God, providing Him the opportunity to address the spiritual condition of the nation and its religious leaders.

(Needed: Prize [optional])

Hand out copies of the reproducible sheet, "The Young, the Bold, and the Stupid." Have kids follow the directions, which should lead to a lot of running around and negotiating. You decide whether kids can initial more than one blank each; this depends on the size of your group. The first person to get all the actions initialed (or whoever gets the most initialed in five minutes) wins. Make sure the winner didn't overspend his or her $10,000 budget. Award a prize if you like. You might want to discuss reactions to items 8, 11, and 12. Note that some actions on the list require boldness, while others require a lack of sense. In this chapter Jesus talks about boldness—in prayer.

DATE I USED THIS SESSION _____ GROUP I USED IT WITH _____

NOTES FOR NEXT TIME _____

_____

_____

1. If the amount of time you pray each day were represented by food, and you could have that much food and no more, what kind of shape would you be in physically? Explain.

2. Have you ever been impressed by the way someone prayed? Who was it and why did it impress you? (Possibilities: Fancy terms; the person's sense of intimacy with God; honesty; emotion; what the person prayed about, etc.)

3. Rather than telling us exactly what to say during our prayers, Jesus concentrated on trying to explain more about the relationship on which prayer is based. Do any of Jesus' insights on God (vss. 5-13) surprise you? Why? (Jesus tells us to "pester" God—we really can't go to Him too often. He assures us that God wants to respond to our requests with only good gifts. Praying should be like talking to a loving father and telling him honestly what we want.)

4. Jesus dismantled some people's idea that Satan was His power source by exposing their faulty logic (vss. 17-26). He then implied that He was the "stronger someone" (vs. 22) who can overcome Satan. If Jesus is stronger than Satan, what difference can that make in (a) the way you handle temptation, and (b) your fears about the future? (We can't claim, "The devil made me do it"; we should stay close to Christ, who strengthens us; our fears of the unknown should be lessened; we can trust His care for us, etc.)

5. How do you think people today are the same as people in Jonah's day or in Jesus' day (vss. 29-32)? How do you think they differ?

6. What do you think is the relationship between light and our eyes (vss. 33-36)? (Light allows the eye to see—without light we're blind. God's light is shining, and we need to open our eyes and let it influence how we see and interpret things.)

7. Jesus was being openly hassled by Pharisees; yet He was willing to accept an invitation to dinner with one of them—even though a conflict arose almost immediately (vss. 37-44). **Who are some of the people who tend to "judge" you unfairly? How could you get together with them in the hope of talking things over?**

8. **In what ways do Christians today act like the Pharisees—perhaps a little too smug or superior to the rest of the world** (vss. 39-52)**?** (Being concerned about how we look to others; being quick to condemn others; being exclusive about who we'll hang out with; being threatened by those who are different from us, etc.) **How about you personally? Do you have any "Pharisee" in you?**

9. **Jesus' bold and honest statements were not appreciated by the Pharisees and religious leaders** (vss. 53, 54). **Has speaking the truth ever gotten you into trouble? Explain.**

Pray the Lord's Prayer (vss. 2-4), but pause after each phrase to ask kids a question they should consider with their eyes closed and heads bowed. **"Father, hallowed be your name." How can you keep God's name holy in the way you talk this week? "Your kingdom come." Do you really hope Jesus comes back this week? "Give us each our daily bread." What can you do this week for people who can't count on daily bread? "Forgive us our sins." What have you done wrong that you haven't confessed? "For we also forgive everyone who sins against us." Who do you need to forgive, and when will you do it? "And lead us not into temptation." What sights or sounds should you avoid this week because you know they'll tempt you?**

The Young the *BOLD*, and the STUPID

Find someone who's willing to do each of the following. Get each willing person to initial the action he or she is willing to do. If you can't find someone who will do an action for free, offer people money. Pretend you have a total of $10,000 to work with.

INITIALS	PRICE (IF ANY)	ACTION
		1. Get a tattoo in a highly visible place.
		2. Don't bathe for two weeks.
		3. Go bungee jumping.
		4. Go skydiving.
		5. Ask the most popular guy/girl in school out on a date.
		6. Tell your P.E. teacher to get a haircut.
		7. Clean your room once a week.
		8. Memorize a Bible verse a week for a year.
		9. Lend $100 to a friend who has a bad memory.
		10. Get your nose pierced.
		11. Sing a solo in church.
		12. Stand on a cafeteria table and witness during lunch.
		13. Eat a chocolate-covered ant.
		14. Do your youth leader's laundry for six months.
		15. Give your school principal a big kiss on the cheek.

LUKE 12

Advice on Investments

CHAPTER ✓ CHECK

Jesus warns His listeners about the "yeast" (hypocrisy) of the Pharisees. Then He tells a parable to emphasize His point. In contrast, He assures His followers that God will take good care of them. In return, they should live their lives in watchful expectation of His return.

OPENING ACT

(Needed: Loaves of bread)

Split the group into teams. Give each team a small loaf of unwrapped, unsliced bread. At your signal, each should try to be the first team to eat the entire loaf. But just before you give the signal, say: **Oh, by the way, watch out for any "surprises" that may be in the loaf of bread.** Then, before kids have time to question, say, **Go!** Though you shouldn't actually put anything in the bread, your warning should cause kids to eat it with caution. When they finish, tell them that you were referring to the *yeast* that was in the bread. Explain that Jesus' followers were also confused when He warned them about the "yeast" of the Pharisees.

DATE I USED THIS SESSION _____ GROUP I USED IT WITH _____

NOTES FOR NEXT TIME_____

_____

_____

1. Have you ever been in a really good mood when you ran into someone in a bad mood, and soon you felt as bad as the other person? (Discuss how certain feelings—especially bad feelings—can spread quickly.)

2. Why do you think Jesus compares hypocrisy to "yeast" (vs. 1)? (Just a little can have a major effect.)

3. Doesn't Jesus seem to contradict Himself when He says, "fear Him [God]," (vs. 5) and then, "don't be afraid" (vs. 7)? Why or why not? (No, He's saying that we should a healthy fear of [respect toward] God, being more concerned about what He thinks of us than about what anyone else thinks. He then assures us that we are of infinite value to God and that He is watching over every detail of our lives.)

4. How can you relate to the person mentioned in verses 13-15? (Have kids share how selfishness has gotten in the way of a relationship.)

5. In what ways do you think people your own age struggle with wanting to "build bigger barns" (vss. 16-21)? (Desire for the right car, the right clothes, all the latest "high-tech toys"; seeing education as the path to big money, prestige, etc.)

6. How are verses 22-34 the solution to the rich man's storage problem? (If you trust God to provide, you don't have to stockpile more than you need.)

7. What things have you worried about this week? When Jesus tells us not to worry (vss. 22-26), does He expect us to simply ignore all these things that concern us? Explain. (No, but in the midst of our concern, He wants us to depend on God. In other words, we should turn care into prayer.)

8. How should Christians distinguish themselves from the rest of the world (vss. 27-34)? (We should always put God first, and trust Him to take care of our everyday needs. As we do, people will see our attitudes and God will get the credit.)

9. What do you think God has entrusted to you to "manage" until He returns (vss. 35-48)? (Our time, talents, money, relationships, etc. Encourage kids to be as specific as possible about their own "assets.")

10. Is the fact that you're getting along with lots of people a sure sign that you're being a good Christian (vss. 49-53)? Why or why not? (Not necessarily. It might just mean that your standards have dropped to the level of everyone else's. True commitment to Jesus is likely to cause division at some point, perhaps between ourselves and some of the people we're closest to.)

11. We don't know exactly when Jesus will return, but we know His return is imminent. So what should be one of our priorities (vss. 54-59)? (We need to "settle our accounts," both with God and with other people.) What outstanding "accounts" do you need to settle with your parents? With someone you've dated? With a brother or sister? With God?

The reproducible sheet, "Locker Inspection," will help kids think about whether they (like the rich man who kept building barns) have a lot more possessions than they really need. Point out that it's easy to see greed and materialism in other people—and easy to try to justify it in one's own life. To reinforce Jesus' teaching, you might consider looking into a weekend (or overnight) youth group project that contrasts the affluence of our own lifestyles with the poverty of other people. One of the more recent ones is "The New Compassion Project," a five-session program available at no charge from: Compassion International, 3955 Cragwood Drive, P. O. Box 7000, Colorado Springs, CO, 80933-9849. Or call 1-800-336-7676.

LOCKER INSPECTION

The rich guy who wanted to build bigger barns for all his stuff (Luke 12:15-21) had a lot more than he needed. Jesus, on the other hand, didn't have much. How about you?

If you had to fit the things you really need into a space no bigger than your school locker, what would you put in it? Here's a list of some things to choose from. Add to the list if you like. Then draw the items you choose in the locker provided, to prove that they'd really fit it there.

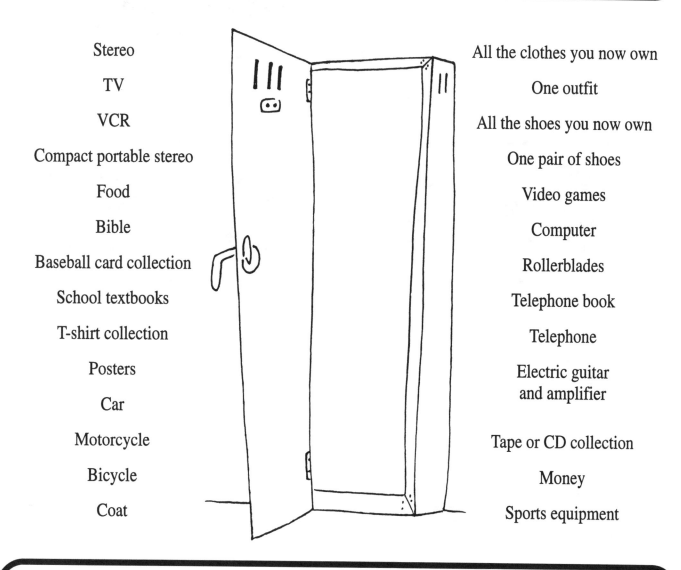

Stereo

TV

VCR

Compact portable stereo

Food

Bible

Baseball card collection

School textbooks

T-shirt collection

Posters

Car

Motorcycle

Bicycle

Coat

All the clothes you now own

One outfit

All the shoes you now own

One pair of shoes

Video games

Computer

Rollerblades

Telephone book

Telephone

Electric guitar and amplifier

Tape or CD collection

Money

Sports equipment

NOW ask yourself:

• Do you have a lot more than you really need?
• Are you planning to get more?
• What does that tell you about where your heart is?

LUKE 13

Figs and Mustard

Hearing of the persecution of some of the Jewish people, Jesus has the opportunity to call all His listeners to repentance. He accompanies His plea with a parable. He then heals a crippled woman on the Sabbath, compares the kingdom of heaven to a mustard seed and to yeast, challenges His followers to find and enter the "narrow door" to God's kingdom, and expresses sadness over the hard-hearted people of Jerusalem.

Have kids get into small groups to read and discuss the reproducible sheet, "Bill and Ted's Amazing Evening." Don't be surprised if kids are unable to agree on the order of responsibility. The story is designed to be difficult, if not impossible, to "figure out." Use this as a lead-in to Jesus' discussion of the often unknown "causes of suffering."

DATE I USED THIS SESSION _____ GROUP I USED IT WITH _____

NOTES FOR NEXT TIME_____

_____

_____

1. When was the last time you thought to yourself, or said to someone, "It's just not fair!"? Do you ever wonder why God allows some people to "get away with" so much, when other people seem to suffer without having done anything wrong?

2. During Jesus' time, people were doing some very real suffering. The Romans had killed some of the Jewish people, and others had died in a tragic accident (vss. 1-5). Jesus had God's perspective on such things. Did He say that these people deserved what they got ? (No. He made it clear they were no more sinful than anyone else. Yet Jesus used these events to emphasize that everyone would die, and those who died without repentance would perish.)

3. Jesus' parable in verses 6-9 is not a well-known one. What do you think Jesus was trying to tell people? (God expects us to be "fruitful" eventually. It's fair to expect a period of growth until we get there, but the time comes when we need to either produce or get out of the way so someone else can.)

4. What does this "fruit" look like? (To "bear fruit," as the phrase is used several times in the New Testament, usually means to bring forth a visible product [or to act on] what you believe. Believers are to bear fruit by obeying God, which involves many kinds of "produce" from sharing faith to developing traits like patience and joy.)

5. Do you see yourself as a "rules-are-meant-to-be-broken" type of person, or a "by-the-book" type of person? Why? How would you have reacted to the events of verses 10-17 if you'd been watching?

6. Jesus really rebuked the synagogue ruler's hypocrisy (vss. 15-17). When was the last time you spoke up against hypocrisy or for love and truth? What happened?

7. What do you think Jesus was saying about God's kingdom in the parable of the mustard seed (vss. 18, 19)? (The kingdom and the tree would start small, but grow into large, fruitful forces.)

8. The parable of the yeast (vss. 20, 21) **was similar. But what was different about it?** (In bread, yeast is the element that works *inside* the dough. The power of God's kingdom would be "spread through" society by people committed to telling their friends and neighbors.) **How could you work like this kind of yeast at your school?**

9. Jesus was making quite a stir, yet only a few of the people who heard Him became dedicated followers (vss. 22, 23). **What can we learn from Jesus' response** (vss. 24-30)? (Not everyone who claims to be a follower of Jesus actually is. We would do well to "enter through the narrow door" quickly, because we don't know how much time we have to make that decision.)

10. Do you think the Pharisees were telling the truth in verse 31? How did Jesus respond to this death threat? (He wasn't scared; He was sad for the people of Jerusalem who would reject Him.) **What can we learn from His response?** (We need to learn to trust God enough to stop focusing so much on ourselves and to think more about others we can help.)

Reread Jesus' parable in Luke 13:6-9—the urgency of becoming fruitful while there is yet time to do so. Explain that many teenagers *will* be dead within a year as a result of bad decisions they will make (drug use, suicide, drinking and driving, etc.). We should do whatever it takes to bear spiritual fruit rather than "waste" space here on earth. Ask each person to think of one thing he or she could do for the kingdom of God during the coming year. If time permits, follow with the actual planting of a tree or flower on the church property (or inside, in a pot). As the plant grows, it will provide opportunities for you to follow up on kids' spiritual progress in the months to come.

BILL and TED'S
AMAZING EVENING

BILL and TED were passing the time Friday evening dropping water balloons from the roof of their apartment building onto unsuspecting pedestrians who walked by. Suddenly, they heard someone scream.

Looking down the street, Bill and Ted saw one of the local gangs beating up and robbing an elderly couple. Had they not been on the roof at that exact time, performing their flying H_2O experiments, they would not have witnessed this terrible event. As they stood up to get a better look, one of their neighbors—grumpy, obnoxious, old Mr. Farley from across the street—spotted them out his window and yelled, "Hey, you kids, what are you doing up there on the roof?"

Unfortunately, one of the gang members heard the neighbor yell, looked up at the roof, and also spotted Bill and Ted—before they could duck out of sight. Realizing that Bill and Ted had witnessed the robbery, the gang broke into a run up the street toward the apartment building.

Meanwhile Bill and Ted practically fell down the fire escape on the back side of the building, and took off down the back alley toward one of their buddies' houses. As soon as Tony, their (supposed) friend, opened the door, Bill and Ted explained their situation and begged to come in and hide. Tony said, "No way, dudes! I just bought a new entertainment system and there's no way I'm gonna let those bogus dudes trash it! Get outta here!"

As Tony slammed the door in Bill and Ted's face, they decided that if ever there was a moment worthy of panic, that moment had arrived. In their hesitation, they were spotted by the gang, which was now rounding the corner of the apartment building and coming up the back alley toward them.

Bill and Ted disappeared around the side of Tony's house, sprinted through the parking lot behind it, and headed for "Big Nick's" place. Big Nick was the biggest, toughest friend they could think of who also happened to live within two blocks. Nick was in front of his house, working on his car, when Bill and Ted spotted him.

It took about ten seconds for Nick to figure out what was going on. By the time the six gang members arrived, Nick was waiting to greet them with his vintage "Hank Aaron" Louisville Slugger and an attitude. Meanwhile, Ted was inside Nick's house, frantically trying to get through to the police. He had been put on hold by the police station switchboard operator, who was on a long-distance call with her mother.

Ten minutes later a squad car was dispatched. As the sirens grew louder, two of the fleeing gang members pulled out guns. Three shots were fired, one of which struck Nick in the chest. Two hours later, while Bill and Ted sat stupefied in the waiting room, wondering why they had ever decided to do the "water balloon thing" tonight, Nick lay critically injured on the operating table.

Now, as a group, you must decide unanimously who, and in what order, has the most responsibility for Nick's condition (#1 = most responsible for Nick's condition, #6 = least responsible for Nick's condition).

_____ Nick   _____ Tony   _____ the gang members   _____ old Mr. Farley

_____ the police switchboard operator   _____ Bill and Ted   _____ the operating surgeon

_____ other : _____

Cost Counters

While eating at a Pharisee's house, Jesus talks about healing on the Sabbath, being humble, and being invited to God's great "banquet" (His kingdom). Then, walking with a crowd, Jesus challenges would-be disciples to think through the high cost of following Him.

(Needed: Snack food)

Pass around an unopened package of Twinkies or chips. Each person has five seconds to make an excuse for *not* taking the food. Anyone who can't come up with a new excuse in time is "out." Award the food to the last remaining player. Then try it again, requiring each person to come up with a more outrageous excuse than the previous player did. Use this later to discuss the excuses people make in verses 18-20 for not accepting the banquet invitation. Ask: **What excuses do people make today for not accepting God's invitation into His kingdom?**

DATE I USED THIS SESSION _____ GROUP I USED IT WITH _____

NOTES FOR NEXT TIME _____

_____

_____

1. If you'd been "spying" on Jesus at the meal (vs. 1), what report would you have made later to your boss? (Probably an angry report that He had "broken" Sabbath rules.)

2. The experts in verse 6 didn't say anything—but what do you think they *felt* like saying? (They probably wanted to accuse Jesus of lawbreaking, but opposing His argument [vs. 5] might have made them look like cold-hearted nit-pickers.)

3. How might the following people try to "exalt themselves" (vs. 11): **(a)** an actor in the school play; **(b)** a girl who's memorized 500 Bible verses; **(c)** a cheerleader; **(d)** a guy who feels he has no friends; **(e)** the center on the football team? How might these people humble themselves instead?

4. Based on verses 12-15, who should you invite to your next party? (Let kids wrestle with the idea of expanding their circle of friends to include those who are rejected by others.)

5. If the kingdom of God is like a feast (vs. 15), why do you think it's so hard to invite your friends? (The food is invisible; others don't know the host; we don't think of it as a feast ourselves, etc.)

6. Why did the host of the banquet get mad (vs. 21) instead of just saying, "Fine! That means more food for the rest of us!"? If the host stands for God, what does this tell you about Him? (He really wants people to come to Him; He's prepared something awesome for us; He doesn't like excuses, etc.)

7. Is Jesus making a point about disabled people in this chapter (vss. 13, 21), or is He getting at something else? (He's probably showing compassion for them and for the poor. But He's also saying that God's chosen people who reject Him are like the first group of invitees—and the Gentiles are like the "outcasts" who are then added to the guest list.)

8. Does Jesus really want us to "hate" our families and our lives (vs. 26)? **Explain.** (Some scholars say He was using hyperbole [exaggeration] to show that our love for Him should be so great that it makes all other loves look like hatred in comparison.)

9. If you were in the crowd and were writing down a "To Do" list as you listened to Jesus, what would be on it? (Let kids pick out at least three key commands and personalize them.)

10. For you personally, what has been the cost of following Jesus so far?

11. How big do you think the crowds were the day *after* Jesus said these things? (Probably smaller, if they understood the tough standards Jesus was setting.)

12. Do you have "ears to hear" what Jesus is saying here? What might plug them up?

Distribute the reproducible sheet, "Cross Carriers," and have kids complete it. As you discuss, pinpoint what would be toughest about each situation—and ask kids to name other heavy crosses they might be asked to carry. Ask: **Did anyone tell you about the "cost" before you became a Christian? If not, do you feel cheated now? Does Christ's command to take up your cross make you feel like getting to work— or trying to get out of this "disciple" thing?**

C R O S S Carriers

"Anyone who does not carry his cross and follow me cannot be my disciple" – Jesus (in Luke 14:27)

How heavy would each of the following "crosses" be for you to carry? Circle the cross that comes closest to showing how tough it would be for you to follow Christ in each situation.

| 1 oz. | 1 lb. | 10 lbs. | 50 lbs. | 100 lbs. |

At the last minute, you have to baby-sit your little sister instead of going with your friends to ride the new monster roller coaster at a nearby theme park.

| 1 oz. | 1 lb. | 10 lbs. | 50 lbs. | 100 lbs. |

On a mission trip to Haiti with your youth group, you don't get to use any indoor plumbing for two weeks.

| 1 oz. | 1 lb. | 10 lbs. | 50 lbs. | 100 lbs. |

Your father decides that your whole family will have devotions together after dinner three times a week.

| 1 oz. | 1 lb. | 10 lbs. | 50 lbs. | 100 lbs. |

You're being pressured to join a gang. The last kid who refused to join was killed in a drive-by shooting.

| 1 oz. | 1 lb. | 10 lbs. | 50 lbs. | 100 lbs. |

You've been going out with this person for six months. You think he/she's perfect for you. But he/she isn't a Christian, and your pastor says you shouldn't be "unequally yoked" (II Corinthians 6:14).

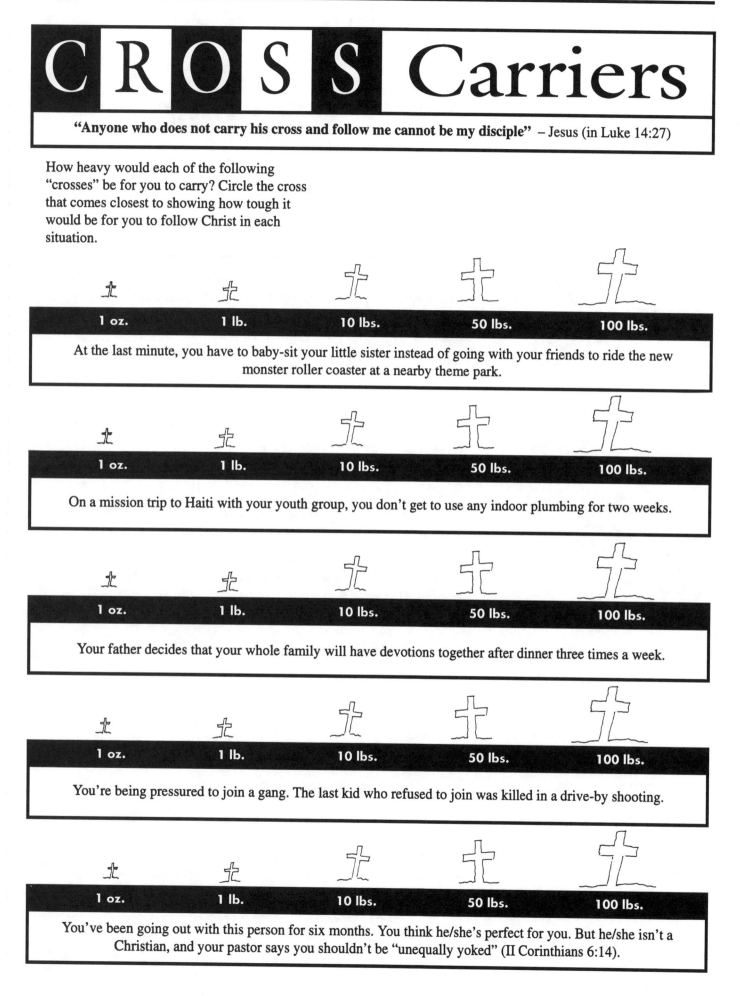

LUKE 15

There's No Place Like Home

With a series of parables, Jesus describes God's concern for those who are "lost." As we relate to the stories of lost possessions, lost money, and lost relationships, we can begin to comprehend how God feels until we "find" our way back where we belong.

(Needed: A few dollar bills)

Before the session, hide a few dollar bills in hard-to-find spots around your meeting place. When kids arrive, let the search begin. Encourage them to "turn the place upside down" to find the money. Let finders be keepers. Refer to this later when you talk about God's interest in finding lost people. But note that while we tend to search out of greed or desperation, God's motive is love.

DATE I USED THIS SESSION _____ GROUP I USED IT WITH _____

NOTES FOR NEXT TIME _____

_____

_____

(Needed: A few coins)

Announce that you're going to play "The Luke 15 Game." Form small groups. Hand out a copy of the reproducible sheet to each small group. Have kids read the game rules. You'll be playing the game during the whole Q&A section. Questions —with responses where appropriate—follow.

1. What is the most valuable thing you've ever lost and never recovered?

2. Describe a time when you got really lost as a little kid. How did you feel?

3. If Jesus came to your school, which people do you think He would hang out with? Why? (Jesus goes where He is invited. He came to save the lost people of the world, not merely the poor, or rich, or middle-class, etc.)

4. What person in your school would be the most likely to win the "Lost Sheep Award"?

5. How do you think Jesus feels about that person, according to verses 1-7? (He loves the person enough to go after him or her, as if he or she were the only one lost.)

6. What's the most money you've ever blown on a date? How did you spend it?

7. In the story of the Prodigal Son (vss. 11-32), **why do you think the younger brother wanted to leave home?** (He felt he was missing out on "real life," he was bored with the same old grind, the grass looked greener "out there," etc.)

8. Why do you think his father gave him the money? (Perhaps because he knew his son had to choose to love him and want to be home with him; he couldn't force that on his son.)

9. Describe a time that you "came to your senses" about something.

10. **What do you think would be going through your mind on the long walk home?** (What's my dad going to say? Are all my farm buddies going to laugh at me? I wonder what they'll be having for dinner? I'm starved, etc.)

11. **Does the father's response to his son's return surprise you at all? What do you think Jesus is saying?** (We've been taught that God will take us back when we repent, regardless of what we have done. But the joyous response of the Father illustrates God's joyous love for every lost child that returns to Him.)

12. **Can you identify more with the older or younger brother? Why?**

13. **Now that the game is over, what's one way you could forgive someone as the older brother needed to? What's one thing for which you need your heavenly Father's forgiveness, as the younger brother did?**

Ask kids to bow their heads and close their eyes as you ask them some questions. Say: **Sure, that prodigal son learned the hard way that "there's no place like home." But what about you? When it comes to your relationship with your heavenly Father, where are you on the path the prodigal son took? At home with the Father, where you belong? Starting to move away from Him, where it seems nothing could be better? On your own, having lost what you had and having picked up a lot of doubts? Down and out, coveting "pig chow"? At a time of decision—to risk going back to your heavenly Father or staying away and staying miserable? Or have you gone full circle and are back with your heavenly Father, where you belong?** If you want to leave a powerful image of the story of the prodigal son, you could play the song by Keith Green, "The Prodigal Son Suite."

THE *L*UKE 15 GAME

INSTRUCTIONS: The player with the most recent birthday goes first, followed by the player on his or her left. Flip a coin to determine how many spaces you move (heads = 1 space, tails = 2 spaces). The first time each person lands on a question he or she must answer it. The first one to the FINISH wins.

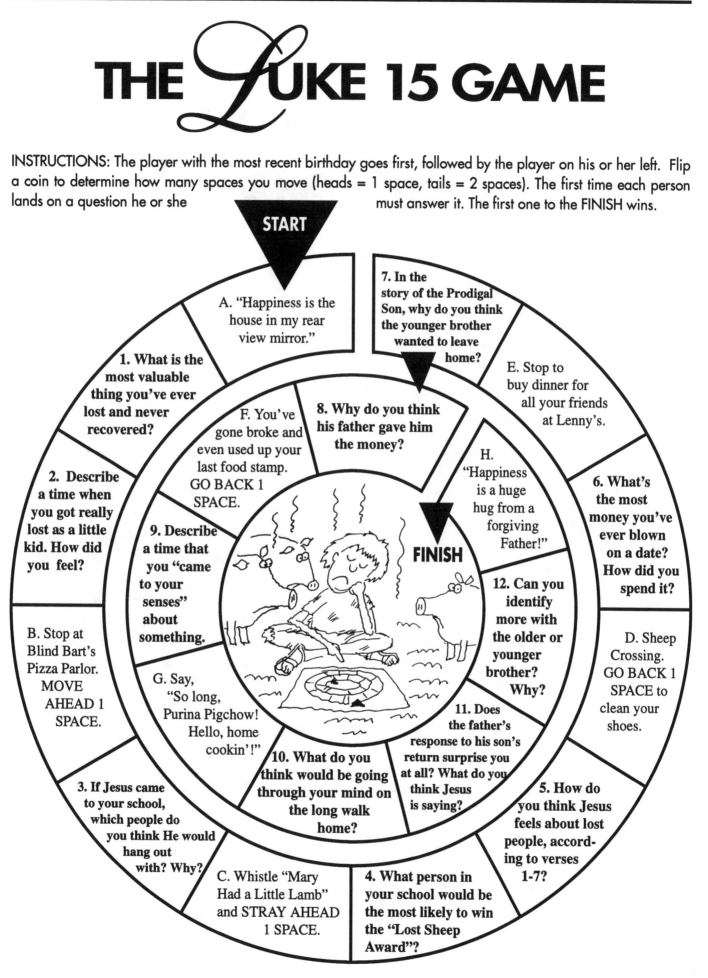

START

A. "Happiness is the house in my rear view mirror."

1. What is the most valuable thing you've ever lost and never recovered?

2. Describe a time when you got really lost as a little kid. How did you feel?

B. Stop at Blind Bart's Pizza Parlor. MOVE AHEAD 1 SPACE.

3. If Jesus came to your school, which people do you think He would hang out with? Why?

C. Whistle "Mary Had a Little Lamb" and STRAY AHEAD 1 SPACE.

F. You've gone broke and even used up your last food stamp. GO BACK 1 SPACE.

9. Describe a time that you "came to your senses" about something.

G. Say, "So long, Purina Pigchow! Hello, home cookin'!"

10. What do you think would be going through your mind on the long walk home?

8. Why do you think his father gave him the money?

7. In the story of the Prodigal Son, why do you think the younger brother wanted to leave home?

E. Stop to buy dinner for all your friends at Lenny's.

H. "Happiness is a huge hug from a forgiving Father!"

FINISH

12. Can you identify more with the older or younger brother? Why?

11. Does the father's response to his son's return surprise you at all? What do you think Jesus is saying?

6. What's the most money you've ever blown on a date? How did you spend it?

D. Sheep Crossing. GO BACK 1 SPACE to clean your shoes.

5. How do you think Jesus feels about lost people, according to verses 1-7?

4. What person in your school would be the most likely to win the "Lost Sheep Award"?

LUKE 16

Gotta Serve Somebody

Jesus tells His disciples the parable of the shrewd manager, which was certain to have caused some confusion and discussion. It is overheard by the Pharisees, causing them to sneer at Jesus' warning against letting money become one's master. But Jesus backs up His point with a hard-hitting story about a rich man and Lazarus.

Form groups of three. Each will act out the following situation; one student plays the teenager, and the other two play the parents. The situation: **A grounded student, wanting to return some library books (but mainly wanting to meet friends at the mall) "borrows" the family car while no one else is home. But on the way back, someone rear-ends the car. A police report is filed, and the insurance company will be calling any minute. The teenager must explain to his or her parents—and get by with as little punishment as possible.** After giving groups a few minutes to prepare their roleplays, have groups act them out for each other. Discuss the "shrewdness" of the teenager in each case. This should set up discussion of the parable of the shrewd manager.

DATE I USED THIS SESSION _____ GROUP I USED IT WITH _____

NOTES FOR NEXT TIME_____

_____

_____

1. Which kind of boss would you prefer to work for: a "by-the-book" person or a "make-up-the-rules-as-you-go-along" type? Why?

2. Jesus told a story about a guy about to lose his job because of his wastefulness (vss. 1-9). This guy was willing to do whatever he could to "land on his feet." What do you think about his business tactics? (The manager was trying to make friends who could help him later. One interpretation is that he was willing to allow his master to lose money. A second is that he simply canceled the "overcharges" that many business people added during this time, which shouldn't have upset the master too much. But either way, the manager was looking out for himself.)

3. Why in the world would the master *commend* the dishonesty of this manager (vs. 8)? (The manager showed initiative, and seemed to realize that some things were more important than money.)

4. So what did Jesus want His followers to learn? That dishonesty pays? (No. We can find spiritual truth in negative examples as well as positive ones. Jesus never praised the dishonesty, yet He suggested that it's wise to sacrifice some money to strengthen relationships [vs. 9], especially for His kingdom.)

5. How can you convince people to trust you with big things (vss. 10-12)? (Never give them reason to question you on little things.) How have you shown on a "little" project that you could handle a bigger one? (Playing on the second string can show you're ready for the first string; baby-sitting your brother or sister can show you're ready to care for other people's kids, etc.)

6. Based on the work you've done in our church so far, do you think the adults would want to give you more to do? Why or why not? If you could take on more responsibility in our church, what would you choose?

7. What "masters" have you served in the past few years? Who was your favorite, and why?

8. Who do you think Jesus' story about the rich man and Lazarus (vss. 19-31) was aimed at? (Probably anyone who sees a need and can help, yet ignores that need.) What insights can we get about hell from this story? (It's a real place; it involves fire and agony; it is eternal separation from God, etc.)

9. How would you summarize the "moral" of this story in one sentence? (Example: We're given one life and instructions for how to live, so we should make the most of every opportunity because it will be too late after we die.)

10. How would you have responded if you'd been a rich person listening to Jesus? What if you were a poor person? (Jesus' words gave hope to poor people. And it would have been simple enough for rich ones to begin to change their ways, though the roots of self-centeredness go deep in many people.)

Have kids look over the "news stories" on the reproducible sheet, "Money Masters." Discuss the stories and the questions in small groups or as a whole group. Opinions may differ on who's serving whom, but emphasize the impossibility of splitting your loyalties. Ask kids to consider where their confidence lies—in what money can do for them, or in what Jesus can do. Note that a good way to find out who you're really serving is to look at your sales slips and your schedule. Where are your investments of time and money really going?

Money Masters

Take a look at the following news clippings, based on true stories. Which of the people in these stories do you think have money (or the things it buys) as their master? Which are serving God instead? Are any of them serving God and money exactly equally?

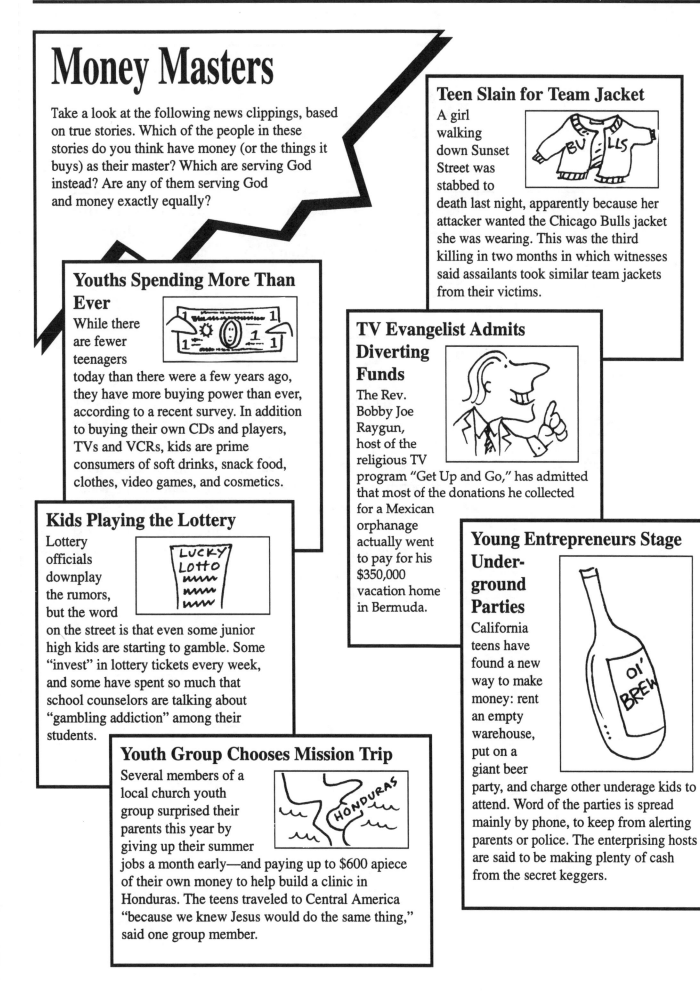

Teen Slain for Team Jacket

A girl walking down Sunset Street was stabbed to death last night, apparently because her attacker wanted the Chicago Bulls jacket she was wearing. This was the third killing in two months in which witnesses said assailants took similar team jackets from their victims.

Youths Spending More Than Ever

While there are fewer teenagers today than there were a few years ago, they have more buying power than ever, according to a recent survey. In addition to buying their own CDs and players, TVs and VCRs, kids are prime consumers of soft drinks, snack food, clothes, video games, and cosmetics.

TV Evangelist Admits Diverting Funds

The Rev. Bobby Joe Raygun, host of the religious TV program "Get Up and Go," has admitted that most of the donations he collected for a Mexican orphanage actually went to pay for his $350,000 vacation home in Bermuda.

Kids Playing the Lottery

Lottery officials downplay the rumors, but the word on the street is that even some junior high kids are starting to gamble. Some "invest" in lottery tickets every week, and some have spent so much that school counselors are talking about "gambling addiction" among their students.

Young Entrepreneurs Stage Underground Parties

California teens have found a new way to make money: rent an empty warehouse, put on a giant beer party, and charge other underage kids to attend. Word of the parties is spread mainly by phone, to keep from alerting parents or police. The enterprising hosts are said to be making plenty of cash from the secret keggers.

Youth Group Chooses Mission Trip

Several members of a local church youth group surprised their parents this year by giving up their summer jobs a month early—and paying up to $600 apiece of their own money to help build a clinic in Honduras. The teens traveled to Central America "because we knew Jesus would do the same thing," said one group member.

LUKE 17

Sink or Swim

Jesus teaches that since sources of sin are so plentiful, His followers must learn to forgive more readily. He also heals ten lepers and teaches about faith, servanthood, and things to watch for in the future.

(Needed: Seven containers; Ping-Pong balls)

Set up seven containers (cans or boxes) into which kids will try to toss Ping-Pong balls. Each container should be about two feet further from the "throw" line than the one before it. As kids compete to see who can get the ball to stay in the most containers, you'll note that most tossers will be weeded out before they can hit the fourth or fifth container. Explain later in the session that this is a little like forgiveness: most of us are willing to forgive a couple of times, but if we're approached "seven times in a day" by the same person, it gets tougher and tougher.

DATE I USED THIS SESSION _____ GROUP I USED IT WITH _____

NOTES FOR NEXT TIME_____

_____

_____

1. Has anyone ever talked you into doing something wrong, or something you didn't really want to do? What happened?

2. Jesus didn't seem to take these "little" offenses lightly (vss. 1, 2). **Why do you think He was so serious about our misleading other people?** (People learn a lot more about us [and what we believe about God] from our actions than from our words. Some disobedience that we might consider harmless is being observed, and perhaps imitated, by friends, little brothers and sisters, etc.)

At this point, pass out copies of the reproducible sheet, "Millstones and Life Preservers." Have kids make their choices. Then discuss the results as a group.

3. Rather than joining someone who's doing something wrong, what might be a better course of action (vs. 3)? (We're supposed to get on the person's case. And then, if the person is sorry, we are to forgive him or her.)

4. Jesus tells us to forgive over and over again every day, if necessary (vss. 3-6). Even His disciples balked at this idea. What's the secret that Jesus gave them in verses 7-10 ? (If we focus on our "rights," it's hard to forgive. But if we see ourselves as servants of God, then serving and forgiving others is just part of our "job." Kids might not normally tolerate much from other people—unless they have jobs as waiters or waitresses and must simply say, "I'm sorry, sir," when a customer complains.)

5. Why do you think God led Luke to include the story of the ten lepers in his Gospel (vss. 11-19)? (Maybe to remind us not to take Jesus' work in our lives for granted, but to thank Him.)

6. How would you feel if you were excluded from society—physically, socially, and spiritually—for many years, and were suddenly able to interact with everyone again? (Compare this with the spiritual parallel Jesus makes possible for us. We are spiritually "unclean," but thanks to Jesus we can stand before God and know we will be accepted.)

7. What do you think Jesus means by "the kingdom of God is within you" (vss. 20, 21)? (People were looking for a physical kingdom—out with the Romans and in with the Messiah. Jesus taught of an unseen, spiritual kingdom. [Some scholars say that "within you" is better translated as "in your midst," so that Jesus was referring to Himself and His availability for people to put their faith in Him.])

8. People were looking for signs, just as people today do. What does Jesus say is one thing we can be certain about concerning His coming (vss. 22-25)? (It won't be a secret that only a few people know about, so we shouldn't be quick to follow people who think they have it figured out. Rather, it will be like lightning—brilliant, unpredictable, and apparent to all.)

9. What will be the similarities between the flood, the destruction of Sodom, and the final return of Jesus (vss. 26-29)? (Everything will seem to be "normal," but suddenly the righteous people will disappear and judgment will fall on those who are left.)

10. Even when judgment is right on their doorsteps, people will be concerned about the wrong things. How can we avoid being like them, or like Lot's wife, who almost escaped judgment, but just couldn't bear to turn completely away from her old life-style (vss. 30-37)? (We should give top priority to Jesus now and continue to do so every day, and we won't have to worry when that time comes.)

(Needed: Edible team prize [optional])

Form teams. Give them five minutes to write down as many things as they can for which they're thankful. Teams will get one point for each item, plus twenty bonus points if they come up with at least one item beginning with each letter of the alphabet. You could have an edible prize for the winning team (just one more item to be thankful for). Encourage kids to reflect this week on all that Jesus has done and, unlike the nine lepers in this chapter, give Him the pleasure of hearing them give thanks.

MILLSTONES AND LIFE PRESERVERS

Read each of the following statements. Decide whether the person making the comment is encouraging someone to stumble or to stand strong. If the comment sounds like it would encourage someone to stumble, circle the millstone. If it sounds like it would encourage someone to stand strong, circle the life preserver. If you're unsure, don't call it anything.

• Hey, it's cool; everybody's tried it at least once.

• Just make up your own mind.

• If you really loved me, you would let me.

• It's OK as long as we're "safe" about it.

• You don't have to do anything you don't want to do.

• There are worse things you could do.

• Come on, it's not that bad.

• How do you think you'll feel about this tomorrow?

• If it feels right, go for it.

• What'll everyone think if you don't do it?

• What'll you think about yourself if you do it?

• Just do to them what you would want them to do to you.

• I guess I can respect your convictions.

• As long as no one gets hurt, what's the problem?

• Rules were made to be broken. Live on the edge, man.

• You're the one who has to live with yourself.

Different Strokes, Different Folks

CHAPTER CHECK

Jesus provides insight on prayer in a couple of creative ways: first by telling a story about a persistent widow and a reluctant judge, and then by telling the parable of the pharisee and the tax collector. He also praises the traits of little children, confronts a rich ruler, tries to prepare His disciples for His death, and heals a blind man.

OPENING ACT

(Needed: Food made with one crucial ingredient left out)

Before the session, make some refreshments with one vital ingredient omitted. (Examples: Cake without baking powder, little sandwiches with no filling, cookies with no sugar, pizza without sauce, etc.) At the start of the meeting, announce that you've brought some great food. List all the ingredients that went into it, making them sound as fancy as possible. Then serve the food. When kids notice a problem, make a show of going back to your recipe and discovering that you left out one "small" item. Like the rich ruler in this chapter, your food lacked just one thing—which made all the difference.

DATE I USED THIS SESSION _____ GROUP I USED IT WITH _____

NOTES FOR NEXT TIME _____

_____

_____

1. What do you think are the most effective ways to wear your parents down when you want something?

2. What do you think about the judge described by Jesus in verses 1-5? (He doesn't sound particularly crooked; yet he seems self-centered and impatient.)

3. When Jesus compares that judge to God, what do you think He's trying to tell us? (Not that God hates being pestered by our prayers, but rather that persistence pays off. If persistence works on self-centered people, think how much more effective it is with a loving God.)

4. Why do you think God wants us to keep coming to Him with our requests? Shouldn't we just give up if we don't get what we ask for? Wouldn't that indicate that His answer is no? (If God answered every prayer request as soon as—or even before—we asked Him, we might never strengthen our faith. Persistence in prayer shows that we are continuing to trust Him for what we need, even when we don't get it right away.)

5. What do you think Jesus is saying in the story of the Pharisee and the tax collector (vss. 9-14)? (Jesus was answering those who thought they were good enough to earn acceptance from God. They were comparing themselves to others based on outward, human standards, rather than on inward attitudes. That's a foolish thing to do before a holy God whose standard is perfection.)

6. When do you recall having thought or acted like the Pharisee, and when like the tax collector?

7. When it comes to impressing God, whom did Jesus single out as a model (vss. 15-17)? Why? (Little children are more trusting, more willing to believe, than many teenagers and adults are. As we become more like this in relation to God, He is pleased.)

8. In contrast to the simplicity of the little children was the complicated life of the rich ruler (vss. 18-25). He thought he was following all the commandments, but what prevented him from being a worthwhile disciple? (His attachment to material things had crept in somewhere along the way. When confronted with needing to do something about it, he was unwilling to do so. Jesus knew that this was the real Master he was serving. Recall Luke 16:1-15.)

9. What would you be most reluctant to sacrifice for Jesus if He were to ask? (Discuss, and then follow up with verses 26-30, where Jesus promises to make up "many times" for any sacrifices made for Him.)

10. Every once in a while, Jesus would try to explain to His disciples that He was going to have to die (vss. 31-34). They had trouble catching on. Yet even today, have you thought through everything His death means to you? Or do you leave that to somebody else? Explain.

11. The blind beggar described in verses 35-43 had a ready answer for Jesus' question, "What do you want me to do for you?" If Jesus asked you the same thing today, how would you respond? And what are some things that you need a little more faith to see clearly?

We can learn a lot from the characters in this chapter—even more if we combine them in new ways. Before the session, cut the situations from a copy of the reproducible sheet, "Strange Skitfellows." Now have a volunteer choose a situation at random. He or she may grab other kids to help with the skit as needed. Distribute the situations randomly until all kids are involved. (If your group is small, do one skit at a time.) After kids perform brief (half a minute to a minute) improvisations, ask group members to compare and contrast themselves to the characters. How are they like each character? How are they different? Remind them that their main goal should be Christlikeness—a pure reflection of Him. Have them think of three specific ways in which they can be more like Jesus this week.

STRANGE

SKITFELLOWS

- -

The persistent widow (vss. 1-6) tries to convince the rich ruler (vss. 18-25) to give her a loan so that she can buy a house.

- -

The self-righteous Pharisee (vss. 11, 12) and the humble tax collector (vss. 13-15) are trapped in an elevator together.

- -

The self-righteous Pharisee (vss. 11, 12) has to babysit the little children (vss. 15-17) and tell them a story.

- -

The humble tax collector (vss. 13-15) tries to collect back taxes from the rich ruler (vss. 18-25). When he can't get the ruler to pay, he goes to the persistent widow (vss. 1-6) for advice.

- -

The little children (vss. 15-17) try to convince the blind beggar (vss. 35-43) that Jesus can heal him.

- -

The blind beggar (vss. 35-43) tries to prove to the self-righteous Pharisee (vss. 11, 12) that Jesus is the Messiah.

- -

The rich ruler (vss. 18-25) tries to explain to the little children (vss. 13-15) why he couldn't do what Jesus asked him to.

- -

Happy Host, Mad Messiah

CHAPTER CHECK ✓

Jesus recognizes and rewards the efforts of Zacchaeus to see Him, and Zacchaeus immediately demonstrates how a relationship with Jesus can make a difference in one's life. Jesus tells a parable about how important it is to use what God has given us for His glory, has His "triumphal entry" into Jerusalem, and drives out the sellers from the temple when He gets there.

OPENING ACT

Select the smallest person in the group. Find out who the person's favorite living personality (athlete, musician, etc.) is. Let another group member act as this "hero." But then have several of your larger members act as "security" for the hero; others can be exuberant fans. The goal of your small person should be to get an autograph from his or her hero. The security people should try to prevent this, and the other "fans" should be swarming around to make things even more difficult. After a couple of minutes of creative effort, the small person (and everyone else) should have a better appreciation for the plight of Zacchaeus in this chapter.

DATE I USED THIS SESSION _____ GROUP I USED IT WITH _____

NOTES FOR NEXT TIME _____

_____

_____

1. Which of your physical features are you most dissatisfied with? How would you change if you could?

2. What problems did Zacchaeus have to deal with (vss. 1-4)? (He was short, and his job as tax collector was not a popular one.) What did he have going for him? (He was wealthy [though this is a good place to point out that lots of money does not ensure happiness].)

3. How did Jesus know to "look up" (vs. 5) when He got to the tree where Zacchaeus was? (Perhaps Zacchaeus was trying to get Jesus' attention. Even if not, it should show us that Jesus is aware of every effort we make to get closer to Him.)

4. When Zacchaeus "went out on a limb" for Jesus, he was rewarded with a personal visit (vss. 5, 6). What are some ways we could go out of our way to get a little closer to Jesus?

5. Knowing Jesus made a real difference in the life and relationships of Zacchaeus (vss. 7-10). He could no longer go around cheating people—at least, not with a clear conscience. How has knowing Jesus changed the way you relate to other people?

6. In the parable Jesus told (vss. 11-27), which of the servants can you identify with most? Why? (Discuss the importance of using the talents God has given us.)

7. Do you feel sorry for the third servant at all? Do you think the master was a little too hard on him? (Point out: the master left specific instructions [vs. 13]; the third servant had an underdeveloped, inaccurate view of his master [vs. 21]; and the master was not angry because the servant had tried and failed, but because he had not even tried.)

8. The master in this parable was accused of being unfair (vss. 24, 25). Do you agree? (Some may think that everyone should be given the same amount of money, talent, or whatever from God. But this parable demonstrates that "whoever can be trusted with very little can also be trusted with much"

[Luke 16:10]. Like it or not, those who invest themselves and their gifts for God's kingdom and glory will understand God better than those who just coast along.)

9. **How do you think Jesus felt as He rode into Jerusalem to the cheers of the crowd** (vss. 28-44)? (It must have been encouraging to hear such praise—even though it was from the "fickle crowd." And Jesus deserved this praise: He always had and always will. Yet His emotions were probably mixed, since He knew that some in Jerusalem would soon be yelling: "Crucify Him!" And He was sad as He told what would happen to Jerusalem in the near future.)

10. **Do Jesus' actions in verses 45 and 46 surprise you? Explain.** (We don't usually think of Jesus as angry. Some scholars believe "those who were selling" would reject the animals foreign visitors brought as unacceptible for sacrifice, in order to sell them new ones, and later resell their original animals to other foreign visitors as "perfectly acceptable" animals.)

11. **Jesus went around teaching people about God, healing the sick, driving out evil spirits, and telling us to love each other. What was the result** (vss. 47, 48)? (His popularity made the Pharisees so jealous and vengeful that they plotted to have Him killed.) **What does this tell you about how people may react if you really obey God?** (We may also experience some suffering at the hands of people who have no respect for spiritual things.)

Have kids look again at the chapter, looking especially at how Jesus responded to each situation He faced. Then hand out the reproducible sheet, "The Jesus Action Figure." Discuss which accessories kids think Jesus would have if He'd come to earth today rather than 2,000 years ago. Point out that Jesus was never "Mr. Tidy and Predictable." He dealt uniquely with each situation He faced—and He will do the same with us, based on our needs. Encourage kids to let the way they see Jesus keep growing and changing as they discover more about Him.

The Jesus ACTION Figure

Which of the following accessories do you think Jesus would have or use if He were walking around on the planet today (instead of 2,000 years ago)? Add a few items of your own if you like. Be ready to explain why you think each item would or would not be used by Jesus.

LUKE 20

Trick or Treat

After having His authority questioned by the religious leaders, Jesus tells a parable of tenants who rejected the authority of the vineyard landowner and abused everyone he sent to check on them. The story angers the religious leaders, who continue to try to trick Jesus—this time with questions concerning taxes and life after death. As a result, Jesus publicly warns His listeners to beware of the teachers of the law.

Tell group members that you want to take an opinion survey. You'll go from person to person, asking questions, and kids can reply only "yes" or "no." Begin with some basic issues: "Do you think the voting age should be raised to 21?" "Do you think MTV has too much sex and violence?" etc. But when you get to a sweet, innocent (and good-natured) group member, pull out a trick question such as, "Don't you think you should stop beating your little sister up?" or "Don't you think you should stop drooling over every new guy (girl) you see?" If these students protest, insist that they answer "yes" or "no." Let them get a little flustered, but don't push too far. Do this just long enough to show that this is exactly the kind of thing the religious leaders were trying to do to Jesus, though He handled Himself better than most of us would in that situation.

DATE I USED THIS SESSION _____ GROUP I USED IT WITH _____

NOTES FOR NEXT TIME _____

_____

_____

1. What questions have you heard that seemed impossible to answer correctly? (Examples: "Who do you think you're talking to?"; "How many times do I have to tell you this?"; "What do you think you're doing?"; "Who do you think you are?")

2. When the religious leaders asked Jesus where He got His authority, why do you think He responded as He did (vss. 1-8)? (They were probably trying to trap Jesus in a "no-win" situation, so He turned the tables and put His accusers in the same spot.)

3. Why do you think the religious leaders were so anxious to make Jesus look bad? (Jesus was a huge threat to their power, had a huge following of devoted people, and had exposed their hypocrisy.) What kind of "religious" question might someone ask if he or she wanted to embarrass you?

4. What do you think Jesus was saying through the Parable of the Tenants (vss. 9-16)? (The Jewish people had a history of rejecting the prophets God sent to set them straight. Now that He had sent His own Son, some of their leaders were going to conspire to kill Him.)

5. Was the death of God's Son going to put an end to the conflict He had with the religious leaders (vss. 17, 18)? (No. After being rejected, Jesus would become a strong force which would cause the fall of those who continued to oppose Him.)

6. If Jesus was such a threat, why didn't His enemies just do away with Him immediately (vs. 19)? (They were afraid of the people's response, since Jesus was so popular—having done so much good.)

7. When direct confrontation didn't work, what else did the religious leaders try (vs. 20)? If someone wanted to discredit your claim to being a Christian, what would be the best time of day to spy on you? Would a spy dig up more "dirt" about you at home or at school? Why?

8. Notice how Jesus answered a true or false question with a multiple choice answer, and taught His questioners a lesson in the process (vss. 21-26). **What was His point?** (That we should give credit to whom it is due—which means God gets ultimate credit for all we have in life.)

9. Other religious leaders came to Jesus with another theological trick question, using a hypothetical situation that would never happen in a million years (vss. 27-40); yet Jesus answered with great authority (and to their satisfaction). Then Jesus asked a question of His own (vss. 41-44). When He had everyone's attention, He gave them a warning (vss. 45-47). **Do you think Christians today need to be more careful of following leaders who are like the Pharisees, or of *becoming* like the Pharisees? Explain.**

10. What are some ways in which you can give "to God what is God's" (vs. 25) even as you meet all your obligations to other authorities in your life? (Discuss specific plans of action.)

Before handing out the reproducible sheet, "Take Your Best Shot," make the following comments: **Jesus really knew how to handle sticky questions. These days if you don't hide your relationship with Jesus, you may face a lot of questions, too—from those who want to discredit you and those who really want to understand what you believe. Here are some examples.** Read one of the questions; then encourage kids to take their best shot at it. Do this with a couple of the questions. Then hand out the sheet. Point out that this sheet barely scratches the surface of defending one's faith. This is simply a place to start thinking about some of these questions.

TAKE YOUR BEST
SHT

Below are some typical questions people ask about Christianity. How would you answer them? (Some hints have been provided.)

What makes you think there is a God out there someplace? You've never seen Him, have you? Don't you just believe God exists because someone told you He did?
(Hint: We all believe in things we've never seen, such as atoms, germs, gravity, etc., simply because "experts" tell us they exist. That argument alone would force us to throw out a lot of what we all believe, simply because we've never experienced it with our senses firsthand.)

How can Christianity be real when there are so many hypocrites who claim to be Christians?
(Hints: First, what is a hypocrite? A phony, a fake. Have you ever seen a counterfeit $13 bill? Why not? Because there are no real ones. Counterfeits only work when there are some real ones around first. Second, real Christians don't pretend to be perfect. They're not; but they are forgiven because Jesus was perfect and was judged in their place.)

If God exists, how could He let so much suffering go on without doing something about it?
(Hint: God didn't create us to be puppets; if God has given us the power to choose whether to love and obey or to disobey Him, mustn't He also let us face the consequences of those choices, good or bad?)

Isn't Christianity just for weak people who need a crutch to lean on?
(Hint: If your leg is broken, you need a crutch. We are disabled by sin. Only a proud fool would reject the crutch he needs in order to walk. Read Revelation 3:15-20.)

Isn't the Bible full of myths and errors, and can't you make the Bible say anything you want it to say?
(Hint: Often this is a smokescreen shielding a lot of ignorance about what's really in the Bible. Have you ever read the Bible? Point out a few of those specific myths or errors that we can scrutinize together.)

What about people who have never heard of Christianity? Will God just send them to hell for their ignorance?
(Hint: Do you really care about those people, or is this a smokescreen to avoid personal responsibility? God will justly deal with each individual. The real issue is: what's your excuse since you have heard? Check out Romans 1:18-20 together.)

Isn't it pretty narrow-minded to say that Jesus is the only way to God? Aren't there many ways to God?
(Hint: Read John 14:6 carefully together and see what Jesus said Himself about those two questions. As C.S. Lewis wrote, "A man who was merely a man and said the sort of things Jesus said would not be a great moral teacher. He would be either a lunatic—on a level with the man who says he is a poached egg— or else he would be the Devil of Hell. You must make your choice. Either this man was, and is, the Son of God: or else a madman or something worse.")

LUKE 21

Checking the Signs

After seeing and commenting on an extremely unselfish gift to the temple, Jesus begins to discuss with His disciples some of the events of the "last days." He warns His friends about coming persecution, false teachers, betrayal by family members, and frightening natural events. He also makes it known that it's possible to "escape all that is about to happen."

(Needed: A wrapped gift of two cents for each person)

Prior to meeting, wrap enough packages so you'll have one per person. Each package should contain just two cents. When students gather, make a short speech about how much you appreciate their faithfulness to each other and their willingness to come to these meetings, and how you would like to show your gratitude. Hand out the presents. Then listen for comments as each person discovers what his or her gift is. Explain that Jesus' disciples didn't think much of two cents either, yet Jesus took special notice of such a gift as He tried to teach them something about giving.

DATE I USED THIS SESSION _____ GROUP I USED IT WITH _____

NOTES FOR NEXT TIME_____

_____

_____

1. Have you ever gotten an inexpensive gift that meant a lot? What and why? (Sometimes a flower picked out of a park or a photo taken in a carnival booth can be more worthwhile than expensive gifts if the giving is spontaneous and from the heart—and especially if the giver is someone special.)

2. If you were casually watching people write big checks and pull out wads of cash to drop into the offering plates, and you suddenly heard the "Clunk, clunk" of two pennies being dropped in, what would you think? (Most people tend to think only in terms of amounts, and not motives.)

3. Why do you think Jesus was so impressed with the small offering of the widow (vss. 1-4)? (What she gave wasn't much until it was compared to what she had. She gave it all—a truly huge gift!)

4. Why do you think Jesus didn't go running up to tell the lady what a good example of giving she was setting? (For one thing, her giving was between herself and God. For another, though we can be sure Jesus notices whenever we do something that honors Him, we shouldn't expect Him to shower down instant rewards every time we choose to do the right thing.)

5. The temple had been built according to precise instructions given by God. Yet when the disciples commented on how nice it was, why do you think Jesus seemed so quick to emphasize that it would be destroyed? (While the temple had been a necessity for the proper worship of God before Christ, from this point on Jesus would be the key. What the priests and sacrifices had symbolized on a temporary basis, Jesus would fulfill permanently. [The temple was destroyed by the Romans in 70 A.D.])

6. As Jesus spoke of future events, the disciples wanted to know more. Of the following signs He gave them to look for, which have you seen take place so far: people deceiving others in the name of Jesus (vs. 8); wars and revolutions (vs. 9); great earthquakes, famines, and pestilences in various places (vs. 11); **persecution of people loyal to Jesus** (vss. 12-15); **betrayal of Christians, even by close family members** (vss. 16-19); **Jerusalem surrounded by armies** (vss. 20-24); **phenomenal changes in nature** (vss. 25, 26); **Jesus returning to earth with power and great glory** (vss. 27, 28)? (Discuss how some of these things are taking place now, how others were fulfilled [in one sense] during the destruction of Jerusalem in 70 A.D., and how others are things we need to continue to watch for.)

7. **When you read about all of this, what do you find yourself thinking and feeling?** (Probably some fear, confusion, a lot of questions, maybe some anticipation, etc.)

8. **In spite of these things, what promises did Jesus leave with His followers** (vss. 14-18, 28)? (He'll provide us with the right words and wisdom; neither suffering nor death can prevent our eternal victory; Christians need not fear, but can look forward to the return of Jesus; etc.) **Do you hope you live to see the time described here? Why or why not?**

9. **With all of these events on the horizon, how does Jesus recommend that we live our lives** (vss. 29-38)? (We should be watchful; dependent on God; not overwhelmed by anxiety; prayerful, etc.)

10. **What do you think we can learn from Jesus' own example about how to face a scary future?** (Jesus knew He would die soon. He wanted to prepare His disciples to be on their own, but He didn't get panicky. Rather, He trusted God as He always had.)

The reproducible sheet, "Don't Miss It," attempts to help your group members think a little more practically about living in light of the return of Jesus. When they finish with the sheets, talk a little about the changes they would make in their lives if they knew for sure that Jesus would be back within a month or a year. Then discuss: **Suppose today were the day Jesus decided to return. If He appeared right here, right now, what do you think He would have to say about us as a group? What single word do you think He might use to describe your life at this point?**

DON'T MISS IT

Here's a list of all sorts of things that you may have thought about doing during your life. But suppose the Lord was to return within your lifetime, possibly very soon. Which of these things (as well as plenty of additions of your own) would you most want to experience or do before Jesus returned?

☐ Play _____
   (sport)
☐ Shoot a bow & arrow
☐ Worship God on top of a
   mountain
☐ Read _____
☐ Go parasailing
☐ Ride a bull in a rodeo
☐ See _____ in
   concert
☐ Be a big brother/sister to a
   needy kid
☐ Get married
☐ Watch the sunrise with a friend
☐ Eat _____
☐ Go snorkeling in the
   Caribbean Sea
☐ Go on a mission trip
☐ Visit _____ (person)
☐ Read my Bible through at least
   once
☐ Speak a foreign language
   fluently
☐ Write _____
☐ Ride a horse through the
   mountains
☐ Hear someone say, "You have
   helped change my life for the
   better"
☐ See the Chicago Cubs play the
   Cleveland Indians in the World
   Series
☐ Meet _____
   (famous person)
☐ Discover _____
☐ Visit _____ (place)
☐ Go sky diving
☐ Help build a home for a
   homeless family
☐ Go to Disneyland or
   Disney World

☐ Go to and finish college
☐ Learn to play _____
   (musical instrument)
☐ Have one really, really
   close friend
☐ Take a trip around the world
☐ Help teach a little kid how
   to read
☐ Swim in a famous body of water
☐ Tell these people about Jesus:
☐ _____ (name)
☐ _____ (name)
☐ _____ (name)
☐ Go to the Super Bowl
☐ Go skiing at some famous
   ski resort
☐ Help stop _____
   _____ (a social
   injustice)
☐ Body surf in the Pacific Ocean
☐ Tell _____ "I love you."
☐ Forgive _____
☐ _____ (other)
☐ _____ (other)
☐ _____ (other)
☐ _____ (other)
☐ _____ (other)
☐ _____ (other)
☐ _____ (other)

One way I hope to make a difference in my world before Jesus returns is:

_____
_____
_____
_____
_____
_____
_____

Betrayer, Prayer, Denial, Trial

As Passover approaches, so does Jesus' death. He has His Last Supper with the disciples, goes out to pray, is betrayed by Judas, arrested, denied by Peter, mocked by the guards, and put on trial.

Before the meeting, cut the 12 questions from a copy of the reproducible sheet, "Pre-Test." When kids arrive, pass questions out at random. (Be sure each person has at least one question; make more than one set if needed.) Have kids mill around, surveying each other to see how many think each question is true and how many think it's false. Don't let kids refer to Bibles yet. Then reveal and discuss the answers. (Answers: All are true except 2, 3, and 8.) Encourage kids to check the answers as you work your way through the chapter.

DATE I USED THIS SESSION _____ GROUP I USED IT WITH _____

NOTES FOR NEXT TIME _____

_____

_____

1. What's the worst you've ever felt because of what someone has done to you, such as breaking a friendship, letting you down at a crucial time in your life, forgetting about you, etc.? What did it do to your relationship with the other person? Did you ever get back together? If so, how long did it take?

2. Why do you suppose Judas agreed to betray Jesus (vss. 1-6)? (There is disagreement among scholars about his exact motive. However, by this time Judas was in some way under the influence of Satan. The issue of money may have been incidental.)

3. What difference did it make that this betrayal took place during the Jewish Passover (vs. 1)? (Passover was a celebration of God's deliverance that involved the sacrifice of a perfect and innocent lamb. The Old Testament institution of Passover had symbolized the sacrifice that Jesus would make.)

4. Why do you think Jesus gave such specific instructions about the Passover preparations (vss. 7-13)? (The disciples didn't realize it, but this would be their "last supper" with Jesus. Perhaps He wanted a special setting to help them remember what He was going to say.)

5. Why do you think Jesus used bread and wine to picture His body and blood (vss. 14-23)? (For one thing, they were daily basics—found in every home and available to all. For another, they could illustrate. In the days before sliced bread, it was "broken" by hand, and grapes were "crushed" to get the juice for wine.)

6. Even as Jesus was preparing to go out and sacrifice Himself for the sins of the world, a debate was taking place among the disciples about which of them was the greatest (vss. 24-30). How might Jesus' advice to them apply to you as well? (Status seeking will never show "differentness" from the rest of the world. But as we practice servanthood, we honor Jesus and become entitled to the rewards He offers.)

7. After some additional warnings (vss. 31-38), Jesus and His disciples went to the Mount of Olives—where Jesus asked them to pray. How would you compare Jesus' intensity in prayer with that of the disciples (vss. 39-46)? With your own?

8. Have you ever been suddenly awakened for a phone call or to do something quickly? How did you feel? Maybe you can relate to the disciples (vss. 47-53). What were some of the things that took place, and what do you think you would have been doing if you'd been there?

9. Why do you think Peter wept so bitterly after denying Jesus (vss. 54-62)? (Maybe he realized, too late, that no amount of suffering as a result of standing up for Jesus would have been as painful as denying Him—especially after he'd told Jesus he'd go to prison or die for Him [vs. 33].)

10. Look at verses 63-71. Have you ever suffered just for telling the truth when it was something the other person didn't want to hear? Explain.

11. Rate in order how bad you feel the actions of the following people were: Judas, Peter, the disciples, the guards, the religious leaders. (This should be difficult. Group members should discover that any offense against Jesus is a sin, and it's difficult to compare levels of sinfulness.)

Ask kids to think about which person or persons in the chapter they can most identify with, and why. Can they relate to Peter's talking big, but then not coming through in the crisis? Or the religious leaders' stubborn resistance to acknowledge Jesus as Lord and submit to Him? Once kids have made their choices, have each person write a note addressed to the person with whom he or she identifies. In the note, the student should explain not just the reason for identifying, but three things he or she will do to avoid being like the Bible character in the future. If you like, collect and mail these notes to the individuals who wrote them one month from now as a reminder of today's reflections.

PRE-TEST

1 True or false: The arrest of Jesus took place during the Feast of Unleavened Bread.
____ people say True; ____ people say False

2 True or false: The Last Supper, contrary to folklore, actually took place in a basement.
____ people say True; ____ people say False

3 True or false: Jesus served the Last Supper, but said nothing about turning it into a way of remembering Him.
____ people say True; ____ people say False

4 True or false: Jesus said His disciples would someday sit on thrones.
____ people say True; ____ people say False

5 True or false: Jesus prayed that He would not have to be crucified.
____ people say True; ____ people say False

6 True or false: An angel appeared in the garden of Gethsemane.
____ people say True; ____ people say False

7 True or false: Jesus' disciples found two swords to defend Him.
____ people say True; ____ people say False

8 True or false: One of the disciples cut off the high priest's right ear.
____ people say True; ____ people say False

9 True or false: Some of those who came to arrest Jesus carried clubs.
____ people say True; ____ people say False

10 True or false: After Jesus was arrested, He was taken to the high priest's house.
____ people say True; ____ people say False

11 True or false: Three times Peter denied being a follower of Jesus.
____ people say True; ____ people say False

12 True or false: When the religious leaders asked Jesus whether He was the Son of God, He said, "You are right in saying I am."
____ people say True; ____ people say False

LUKE 23

It's Over

Jesus is taken before Pilate, sent to Herod, and then back to Pilate again. Pilate wants to release Jesus and execute Barabbas instead, but the people won't hear of it. Consequently, Jesus is crucified. As He dies, people gather to mock Him. But one of the criminals crucified with Him experiences the depth of God's forgiveness. Shortly thereafter, Jesus dies and is buried.

(Needed: Bag of candy)

Pick a good-natured group member. Tell the other kids that you're trying to get some "dirt" on this person. What can they tell you about him or her that's bad? As kids comment, reward them with candies from your bag. Give one candy for "tame" information and two for "juicier" tidbits. See how far kids are willing to stretch the truth (or even lie) to earn these rewards. Make sure things don't get hostile or out of control, however. Finish by rewarding your "victim" with the rest of the candy. Use this activity to show how accusations intensify—and truth gets twisted—with a crowd mentality that feeds on negative comments.

DATE I USED THIS SESSION _____ GROUP I USED IT WITH _____

NOTES FOR NEXT TIME _____

_____

_____

1. Has anyone ever told an out-and-out lie just to get you in trouble? How would you handle it if someone did?

2. When Jesus went on trial before Pilate, how did people distort the truth about Him (vss. 1, 2)? (They lied about what He had said about paying taxes [Luke 20:25]. They accused Jesus of "subverting" the nation and being a serious political threat to Rome.)

3. Pilate had the authority to release Jesus, and he didn't believe Jesus deserved to die. So why didn't he let Jesus go (vss. 3-5)? (The pressure Pilate felt from the people influenced his decision.) How do we let other people keep us from making decisions we know would be best?

4. Pilate found a loophole, or so he thought. Since Jesus was from Galilee, that put Him in King Herod's jurisdiction. Pilate had Him transferred (vss. 6, 7). What hard decisions might you want to put off or dump on other people?

5. Herod's only interest in Jesus was having someone who could entertain him (vss. 8-12). Do you know anyone who's only interested in a youth group "for the fun of it"? What is that person missing?

6. Herod sent Jesus back to Pilate, who still didn't want to condemn Him to death. Pilate had to take a stand or risk angering the large crowd. As the noise got louder, Pilate's resistance weakened until he finally gave those present what they wanted (vss. 13-25). What are some decisions kids might make in the heat of the moment, under pressure, that they'd regret later? (To have sex; to talk back to parents; to quit school, etc.)

7. A person from the crowd, Simon of Cyrene, was recruited to help Jesus carry His cross (vs. 26). Have you ever been "talked into" doing something "for Jesus" that you didn't really want to do, but discovered later that it was worth your effort? (Examples: Missions projects, nursing home visits, etc.)

8. Jesus was sad about the destruction He knew would come to Jerusalem (vss. 27-31). He was physically exhausted. He was a sinless man, stripped and nailed to a cross between two common criminals. If you were in this situation and had the power Jesus had, what would you have done? What did Jesus do? (The fact that Jesus chose to pray for the forgiveness of these people should motivate us to greater patience, love, and self-sacrifice.)

9. Look at the responses of the two criminals (vss. 32-43). What does this passage suggest to you about salvation? (It's each individual's choice; it's never too late to make that choice; Jesus is eager to forgive a repentant person; works are not a prerequisite to salvation—the thief could do nothing, yet was accepted by Jesus.)

10. How did Jesus' death make a difference to the centurion (vss. 44-49)? To Joseph of Arimathea (vss. 50-56)? (Both were moved to show faith in words and actions.)

11. How have you responded to Jesus' death? Do you pretty much take it for granted? Are you trying to gather more evidence to convince yourself that it was a big deal? Has it changed the way you live your life? Explain.

Until we feel grief over the death of Jesus, we can't fully appreciate His resurrection. The reproducible sheet, "The Death of a Friend," encourages kids to respond to Jesus' death as they might to that of a friend or family member. When kids finish, have them share answers as they're willing. Discuss how Jesus' friends and family must have felt during the three days He was in the tomb. Assure kids that Jesus understands when we grieve for friends and relatives, too, and that He provides "new life" beyond the feelings of loss and hurt that are a necessary part of grieving.

The Death of a Friend

For a few minutes, try to forget the way you usually think of Jesus' death. For these few minutes, you are a close friend of Jesus—one of His disciples. For three years you have walked and worked just a few feet away from Him. You've eaten a lot of roast lamb and broiled fish with Him, shaken your head in confusion at some of His stories, and snickered behind the backs of the Pharisees when Jesus cut them off with a brilliant answer. Jesus is not only "the Teacher" to you—He is the best friend you've ever had.

❖

You were looking forward to so many adventures with Him. There were so many more things you wanted to learn. But suddenly, more suddenly than you could have thought possible, it all ended. There were the soldiers, the kiss of that traitor Judas, and all at once you lost your nerve. Ashamed, your face burning, you ran into the night—leaving your best friend to face brutal beatings and a slow, agonizing death.

❖

They buried Him yesterday. You didn't sleep more than a few minutes last night. You feel numb, exhausted. You wonder when the shock will wear off and the real pain will start. Already you've cried more than you'd cried in the first 31 years of your life; your eyes are red and your throat is throbbing.

You sit, staring out the window, and think:

The first three words that come to mind when I think of Jesus' death are . . .

More than anything else, I think Jesus will be remembered for . . .

Jesus' death seems so unfair because . . .

If Jesus hadn't died so soon, I was hoping He and I could . . .

Other people carried His cross, gave Him a tomb. All I can do is . . .

I wish I had told Him before He died that . . .

His death makes me think about my own death, and that . . .

I don't see how any good can come out of Jesus' death, except maybe . . .

I guess the next thing I'll do is . . .

LUKE 24

A Great Way to Start the Day

CHAPTER CHECK

When a group of women go to anoint Jesus' body, they find an empty tomb instead. Angels tell them that Jesus has risen from the dead, and the women hurry to tell Jesus' disciples. The disciples don't believe them. But Jesus Himself later appears to the disciples, after first walking (unrecognized) with two others on the road to Emmaus. He seeks to explain what has happened, and then ascends into heaven.

OPENING ACT

Before the session, get one of your kids to agree to "disappear" early in the meeting. This person should be seen by most of the group, but should then slip away and find a good hiding place. Act as if you're ready to get things going, but keep finding reasons why you can't until the missing person shows up. (Examples: He or she was supposed to give the opening announcements, pump up the volleyball, bring the refreshments, etc.) Eventually have the group search for the missing person. When he or she is finally discovered (or comes out of hiding), discuss what it must have been like for Jesus' friends to "get things going " after His death. They must have depended on Him for so much; it must have been difficult to think about beginning life again without Him.

DATE I USED THIS SESSION _____ GROUP I USED IT WITH _____

NOTES FOR NEXT TIME _____

_____

_____

Q&A

1. On a scale of 1 to 100 (100 highest), what do you think the stress levels of the women were as they went to Jesus' tomb? Why?

2. How would you feel if you went to the cemetery to put flowers on someone's grave, and when you got there all you found was a big hole beneath the headstone? How do you think the women (vss. 1-3) felt when all they found was an empty tomb? (Probably they first thought that someone had moved the body or otherwise tampered with the grave.)

3. On top of their confusion, the women were in for a shock (vss. 4-8). Have you ever been told something that was "too good to be true"? What made the women at the tomb believe what they were told? (The radiant appearance of two angels would be pretty convincing.)

4. Why do you think the disciples didn't believe the women's report (vss. 9-11)? (Perhaps it sounded like "nonsense" to them because during Jesus' ministry they had seen little indication of angelic activity. The report of the women would be hard for any of us to believe.)

5. Why do you think Peter got up and ran to the tomb (vs. 12)? (One of the last things he had said to Jesus was that he was willing to die for Him [22:33]. Then he had denied Jesus three times, and the next day Jesus was dead. Maybe Peter wanted to ask forgiveness.)

6. As Cleopas and his friend walked to Emmaus (vss. 13, 14), they were disappointed because Jesus, whom they'd hoped was the Messiah, had died. Yet they were hopeful because of the women's report of the angels and the empty tomb. When you begin to doubt that God is there, what are some of the "signs" that keep you hopeful? (Examples: The beauty of creation; the written Word of God; the difference God is making in the lives of other Christians, etc.)

7. Eventually the travelers discovered that Jesus had been with them all along, and they just hadn't realized it (vss. 15-31). How does this happen to us? (The *fact* that

Jesus is always near gets masked by our *feelings* due to fatigue, worry, sadness, stress, disappointment, etc.)

8. **Do you ever get as excited about Jesus as these two travelers did** (vss. 33-35)**? Why or why not?** (When Jesus becomes real to us, our "hearts burn within us" and we are eager to spread the news that Jesus is alive.)

9. **When Jesus reappeared to His disciples, He helped get them on the right track by discussing His relationship to them in the present** (vss. 36-43)**, the past** (vss. 44-47)**, and the future** (vss. 48-53)**. When in the past was your relationship with Jesus strongest? What's one thing He seems to be doing in your life now? What do these things motivate you to do in the near future?**

(Needed: Easter songs and tape player [optional])

When the resurrection of Jesus Christ becomes real for us, it gives us a new perspective. Let kids look over the cartoons on the reproducible sheet, "Right Questions, Wrong Answers." Ask: **Have you ever felt like any of these kids? Why?** Then have kids complete the four statements and share them if they're willing. If you can, follow up with a time of celebration for everything Jesus' resurrection makes possible. Since there are so many contemporary Christian songs about the resurrection, you might want to bring a few to play, too.

Here are some questions asked in the last chapter of Luke. But you won't find these answers in the Bible. They're like answers some of us might have given. Look them over. Then, from your own viewpoint, complete the statement that follows each answer.

Because Jesus is alive, the best attitude
I can have about death is:

Because Jesus is alive, the best thing
I can tell my friends is:

Because Jesus is alive, the best thing
I can do with my Bible is:

Because Jesus is alive, the best thing
I can do with my problems and doubts is:

JOHN 1

A Picture Paints a Thousand Words

CHAPTER ✓ CHECK

While Matthew and Luke began their Gospels with the birth of Jesus as a baby, John gives another perspective. He describes Jesus as existing with God the Father "in the beginning." The Christmas story, then, is when "the Word became flesh." And from that point, John quickly moves into Jesus' ministry: His relationship with John the Baptist, His role as the Lamb of God, and the call of His disciples.

OPENING ACT

Give one member of your group a copy of the reproducible sheet, "Carbon Copy?" Have him or her try to describe what it looks like by following the rules listed on the sheet. As the volunteer describes the drawing, the rest of the group should try to reproduce it on paper. See if anyone can guess what it's supposed to be, then compare drawings to the original. This activity illustrates why "the Word became flesh and made His dwelling among us." Words alone would have never been enough to show us what God is like.

DATE I USED THIS SESSION _____ GROUP I USED IT WITH _____

NOTES FOR NEXT TIME _____

_____

_____

Q&A

1. When was the last time you tried desperately to communicate with someone, but just couldn't seem to get through? How did you feel?

2. What do you think it means when Jesus is called "the Word" (vss. 1, 14)? (In the past, God communicated through the written word, and the spoken words of prophets. Now He is taking the ultimate step of communicating with us by coming to live among us.)

3. What do we learn about "the Word" right away (vss. 1-5)? (The Son has always existed; He is God, but is distinguishable from the Father; He was involved in creation; He has an influence on the "darkness" of humankind, but people do not always understand Him, etc.)

4. The John mentioned in this chapter is John the Baptist—not John the apostle who wrote the Gospel. What was John the Baptist's relationship with Jesus, and in what ways do we carry on a similar relationship (vss. 6-9)? (John the Baptist prepared the way for others to believe in Jesus. So should we.)

5. Why do you think it was necessary for "the Word" to become flesh (vss. 10-18)? (Jesus had to show us exactly what the unseen God was like. His coming was necessary for us to become God's children and receive His grace and truth. Jesus was able to answer questions, display God's power, and show God's love first-hand.)

6. John the Baptist was such a bold speaker that people confused him with the Messiah who had been prophesied (vss. 19-28). How would you feel if someone confused you with Jesus? Why?

7. John the Baptist clearly testified that Jesus is "the Son of God" (vs. 34). Yet John also calls Him "the Lamb of God" (vss. 29, 35). Why did John use such a powerless animal as an illustration? (Jesus came in human form to be a sacrifice for all people. While He had great power, He would not use it for Himself. Jewish people would be able to identify with the image of a sacrificial lamb.)

8. John the Baptist had already begun to teach disciples, and he steered some of his followers toward Jesus when He came along (vss. 35-39). **Suppose you were one of these disciples introducing yourself to Jesus for the first time. What would you say?** (Contrast student responses with the disciples' not-so profound question: "Where are You staying?")

9. One of these disciples was Andrew, who then became Jesus' disciple. **How much do you know about Andrew? How much do you know about Simon Peter?** (Let students respond. Then show that even though Andrew is overshadowed in the Gospels by Peter, anything to Peter's credit can be traced to this action [vss. 40-42].)

10. **What resistance did Jesus face from Nathanael, and what can we learn from the way He dealt with it** (vss. 43-51)? (Nathanael felt nothing good could come out of the obscure village of Nazareth. In spite of Nathanael's basic prejudices, Jesus' insight into his unique character quickly won him over. We can let rejection prevent us from developing strong relationships, or we can focus on the other person's strengths and try to get past his or her defenses.)

Make a list of all the things this passage teaches about Jesus (He helped create the world, He always existed, He gives life, He is light, etc.). Then note the similarities between Andrew and Philip's initial response to Jesus in verses 41 and 45 (they both invited someone else that they cared about to meet Jesus). **Suppose you just met Jesus for the first time. Who would you most want to have meet Him, too? From the list we made, what characteristic of Jesus do you think would mean the most to this person? How can you introduce him or her to Jesus?**

Try to get the rest of your group to draw this object without:
- Telling them what it is
- Using any letters or numbers
- Using any hand gestures
- Having them ask any questions

Here's what you can do:
• Describe the shapes   • Describe the sizes of the shapes   • Describe the position of the shapes on the page

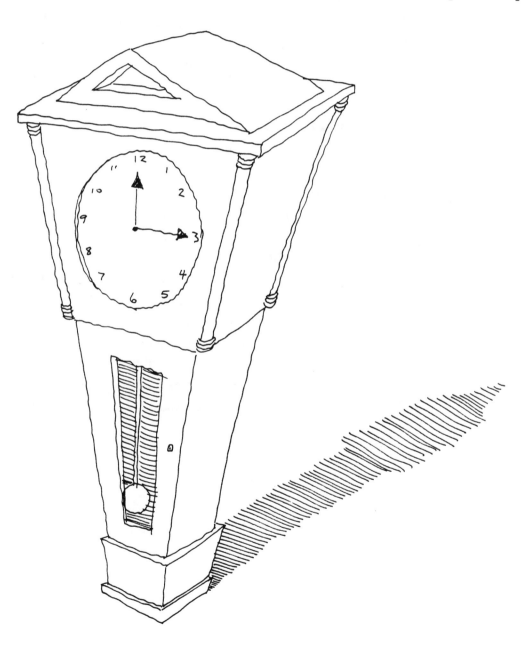

JOHN 2

Just Add Water

Jesus performs His first miracle: turning water to wine at a wedding in Cana. He also shows that there is more to His ministry than miracles and popularity as He physically drives the money changers out of the temple. From this point on, some people will grow more loyal to Him while opposition mounts among others.

(Needed: An assortment of "just add water" mixes)

Serve refreshments by seeing how many different things your group can "turn water into." Use prepackaged mixes to "create" instant lemonade, tea, hot chocolate, and so forth. You might even take this one step further by having a microwave on hand and seeing how many foods you can add to the list (oatmeal, rice, pancakes, etc.). If you want, make a game out of it by blindfolding volunteers and having them guess what they are tasting. As you sit around and sip your creations, ask: **Do you think Jesus' miracle of turning water into wine was similar to what we have done, or different? Why?** As students respond, lead into the facts of the story.

DATE I USED THIS SESSION _____ GROUP I USED IT WITH _____

NOTES FOR NEXT TIME _____

_____

_____

1. What's the most embarrassed or uncomfortable you've ever been as a host or hostess, or as a guest at someone else's party?

2. Does it surprise you that Jesus and His disciples would be invited to a wedding (vss. 1, 2), **or that they would go? Why or why not?** (Some people think of Jesus as such a serious, spiritual person that He would never enjoy social events. Jesus shows that it is quite possible to be "spiritual" in the midst of "social" activities.)

3. Some of the wedding feasts during this time could last a week, so it's not out of the question that someone would run out of wine. But what do you think the host's options were then? (The only other drink available in such quantities was water—not a very festive drink. We don't know of the host's financial status; even if he could have paid for more beverages, it's not like he could run out to the 7-11 at a minute's notice. The most probable option was sending the people home and suffering the embarrassment.)

4. Since Jesus hadn't performed any miraculous signs yet (vs. 11), **why do you think His mother was so eager that He get involved** (vss. 3-5)? (At this point in His life, perhaps she was the person who knew Him best. The better any of us get to know Jesus, the more we discover what He is capable of doing.)

5. What are some of the significant things you notice about Jesus' first miracle (vss. 6-11)? (It was in response to a social need rather than a physical or spiritual one; it was done on a large scale [six jars holding 20 to 30 gallons each]; it was a work of high quality, etc.)

6. Does this passage imply that it's okay for Christians to drink alcoholic beverages? (Many kids will be curious about this, so you might as well address it head-on. This is an issue where opinion is divided, so you should stress your own church's position. Keep in mind that in Jesus' day, beverage options were quite limited: it was either water or wine for most occasions. Some people hold that the wine referred to in these verses did not lead to intoxication, but was rather a type of unfermented grape juice. Others suggest that these verses do support the practice of drinking in moderation. In either case, those under the legal drinking age should not be drinking—even in moderation!)

7. **Why do you think Jesus became upset with what He saw in the temple** (vss. 12-14) **and took immediate action** (vss. 15-17)**?** (Some scholars believe that "the money changers" skimmed off profits while converting foreign visitors' money into "proper temple currency," and/or rejected the animals these visitors brought as unacceptable for sacrifice, so they could sell them new ones, and later resell their original animals to other foreign visitors as "perfectly acceptable" animals.)

8. **If Jesus "sat in" on our church service and observed each of our activities, how do you think He would respond? Why?**

9. **Jesus tried to explain over and over that He would eventually be killed as a sacrifice for the sins of the world** (vss. 18-25), **though apparently no one caught on until after His death. When did you first "catch on" to this truth, and what seemed to be the thing that made "the light come on" for you?**

10. **Verse 25 says that Jesus "knew what was in a man." What do you suppose this refers to?** (He knows our hearts—our attitudes and motives. Jesus realized how fickle people can be. It was too soon to entrust Himself to too many people.)

The reproducible sheet, "Temple Cleaning" will help group members evaluate the areas of their lives where they might need to "clean house." Since this is kind of personal, don't force anyone to share what he or she has written. Stress the fact that we see two sides of Jesus in this chapter: the temple-clearing side and the celebrating side. **What are some things that Jesus would celebrate if He came to visit this group today?**

In this chapter we see Jesus clearing out the temple. Did you know that your body is also a temple? (See I Corinthians 3:16 and 6:19.)

In the diagram below, list some things that might need to be cleared from your temple. For example, maybe it's a certain television show you watch, some type of junk food you know you should give up, or a hateful feeling toward someone.

Temple Cleaning

What you think:

What you look at:

What you listen to:

What you say:

What you do:

What you feel:

What you swallow:

Where you go:

JOHN 3

"Nic" at Night

Nicodemus, a Pharisee, visits Jesus at night to find out more about Him. In this much-quoted passage of Scripture, Jesus speaks of the need to be "born again," and the extent to which "God so loved the world." Later, John the Baptist explains to his disciples that they should not be upset to see many of their followers going to Jesus, because Jesus is the one who provides eternal life.

Play "The Eliminator" game on the reproducible sheet, but each time the number of players begins to get depleted, call "everybody back in." Do this a couple of times. As you continue to let people back in, some may begin to question the purpose of the game if you never "eliminate the losers" to find a "winner." Point out that Christianity is similar: God gives everyone a chance to get back "into the game" during his or her life—by grace—through Jesus.

DATE I USED THIS SESSION _____ GROUP I USED IT WITH _____

NOTES FOR NEXT TIME _____

_____

_____

1. If you could have a private, face-to-face conversation with Jesus, what would you want to talk about? What feelings would you have as you prepared to meet with Him?

2. Why do you think Nicodemus went to Jesus at night (vss. 1, 2)? (Maybe to avoid detection—and possible embarrassment—or to bypass the crowds and have an in-depth discussion. He had some big questions to ask Jesus, but he was a Pharisee—a religious leader who was supposed to have "all the answers.")

3. Nicodemus recognized Jesus' wisdom and power. In reply, Jesus said, "No one can see the kingdom of God unless he is born again" (vs. 3). Why do you think He responded that way? (Maybe to cut the small talk, to knock Nicodemus off balance and spark his curiosity, to challenge his thinking, etc.)

4. The term, "born again" is familiar to many people today. Suppose someone asked you to explain it. What would you say? (Some people use the term to describe any type of life-changing event like falling in love or some type of vague religious experience. But Jesus is talking about something deeper. Being born again begins with a sense that we were originally born with a sinful nature and are in need of a Savior. By the power of the Holy Spirit, we claim responsibility for our own sin, turn away from it, and trust in Jesus for salvation.)

5. Nicodemus's question in verse four really exposed his ignorance, but it also showed Jesus how much he wanted to understand. Then Jesus clarified His statement (vss. 5-21). When you don't understand something about Jesus, God, or the Bible, what do you do?

6. What did Jesus mean about the time when "Moses lifted up the snake in the desert" (vs. 14)? (If students are unfamiliar with the story, have someone read Numbers 21:4-9 and explain the symbolism Jesus refers to.)

7. The decision about whether or not to believe in Jesus is a crucial one. The options are simple: You do or you don't. But what are the long-range results of each decision (vss. 16-21)? (Belief in Jesus results in eternal life [vs. 16], assurance of salvation [vs. 17], and a lifestyle of confidence. Rejection of Jesus results in condemnation [vs. 17], perishing [vs. 16], and fear [vs. 20].)

8. What kinds of character qualities do you see in John the Baptist (vss. 22-30), **and what can we learn from him?** (John was humble and willing to submit to God. He shows us that we don't need to put ourselves first to experience joy.)

9. In what areas of your life has Jesus become greater as you've become less (vs. 30)? In what areas do you still struggle with wanting to prove that you're the greatest?

10. As John the Baptist continues with his explanation to his disciples (vss. 31-36), he echoes something Jesus had told Nicodemus: Whoever believes in Jesus has eternal life (vss. 15, 36). **Why do you think he says "has" instead of "will have?"** (Putting one's faith in Jesus begins a relationship with God at that point, not after we die.)

11. Have you begun living as if you have eternal life, or are you waiting till later? Explain.

This chapter contains one of the most famous verses in the Bible—John 3:16. Many group members have probably memorized it, or have seen it displayed at a sporting event. But how well do your kids know what the verse means? Read the following situation and discuss the questions. **During the Super Bowl, a guy in a bright orange fright wig holds up a John 3:16 sign every time the TV camera focuses on the end zone where he's sitting. What would you say to the following people: A friend who's watching the game and wonders what the big deal is with "John 3:16" anyway? A friend who comments that the guy in the wig is obnoxious? The guy holding up the sign? If you could hold up any sign at the Super Bowl to tell the world about Jesus, what would your sign say?**

The ELIMINATOR

INSTRUCTIONS:

Pair off (if you have an odd number of people, form one group of three). Once everyone's paired, have your leader call out a number between 1 and 20. Look up that number and decide which person in each pair the statement applies to. That person is still "in." The other is "out." If there's a tie, both stay "in." People still "in" pair up again, another number is called, and so forth until only one is left. That person is the winner.

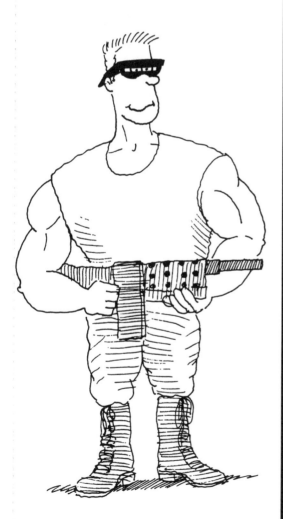

1	2	3	4
Person with the most siblings.	Person who most recently saw a movie starring Kevin Costner.	Person with the oldest living relative.	Person who most recently went skiing (water, cross-country, or downhill).
5	**6**	**7**	**8**
Person whose family drives the oldest car.	Person with the smallest fingernail.	Person whose first name starts with a letter closest to "Z".	Person with the least money with him/her.
9	**10**	**11**	**12**
Person wearing the most red.	Person with the most pets.	Person with the fewest speeding tickets.	Person who's been to the fewest states outside his/her home state.
13	**14**	**15**	**16**
Person wearing the most green.	Person who's older.	Person who most recently ate at a fast food place.	Person whose birthday is closest to Christmas.
17	**18**	**19**	**20**
Person wearing the least jewelry.	Person who's had the most cavities in his/her teeth.	Person with the fewest letters in his or her full name.	Person who lives farthest from where you are right now.

Well Spoken

At a well in Samaria, Jesus meets a woman who is responsive to His teaching. The traditional prejudices between the Jews and the Samaritans are forgotten as gradually the woman puts her faith in Him. She introduces Him to many of her neighbors, who also believe. Later, Jesus heals the son of a royal official.

(Needed: Jigsaw puzzle[s])

Divide your group into at least two teams. Give each team a jigsaw puzzle. Turn all the pieces face down and see which team can assemble the most pieces within a given time limit. Then let groups turn their pieces face up and continue. Set another time limit. Finally, let them see the puzzle box, so they know what their pictures look like. Set a final time limit. After announcing a winner, discuss how difficult it is to do some things with just a little bit of information. But after you collect enough facts, the answer/solution seems very clear. As you study the woman at the well, observe how she collects bits of information about Jesus and eventually sees who He really is.

DATE I USED THIS SESSION _____ GROUP I USED IT WITH _____

NOTES FOR NEXT TIME _____

_____

_____

1. Describe a time when you were extremely thirsty. How long did you go before you quenched your thirst? What did you drink?

2. The Samaritans were descendants of Jews who had intermarried with foreign nations centuries before, and conflict between the Jews and the Samaritans is mentioned in a number of places throughout the Bible. Jesus could have bypassed Samaria, as many other Jews would have. Why do you think He didn't (vss. 1-4)? (This single visit would have long-lasting impact, both on this community where He stayed, and on His disciples.)

3. Who are some people you would equate with "Samaritans" today—groups who are usually looked down on or outcast? (Certain ethnic groups; visibly disabled people; old people, etc.)

4. If Jesus hadn't wanted to talk with this "foreign" woman (or if He had been many of us), what "good excuses" could He have come up with (vss. 5-8)? (It was socially inappropriate for a man to talk one-on-one with a woman; He knew of this woman's bad reputation; it was the middle of a long, hot day, and He was probably tired; His disciples wouldn't understand; etc.)

5. But Jesus didn't make excuses as He began a conversation with the woman. What can we learn from the way He started the dialog (vss. 7-15)? (Evangelism is more effective as we find common ground—physical, emotional, or otherwise—with the people we talk to. Jesus asked for a drink of water, and then told her that He had a spiritual "thirst quencher" to offer in return.)

6. How would you feel if someone started telling you about deeply personal things in your life that you thought were well hidden? Would it make a difference whether or not you thought the person was accusing you of something? (Compare answers with the facts of the story [vss. 16-19].)

117

7. The woman's responses to Jesus show her growing level of belief: "a Jew" (vs. 9), "Sir" (vs. 11), "a prophet" (vs. 19), "Could this be the Christ?" (vs. 29) After thinking through these things herself, did she leave it up to others to reach the same conclusion on their own (vss. 27-30)? What can we learn from her response? (She was quick to share the truth she had discovered—at least to "connect" other people with Jesus. Of course, it was then up to each person to make his or her own decision [vss. 39-42].)

8. The disciples had no idea what was going on (vss. 27-38), but many Samaritans put their faith in Jesus (vss. 39-42). To what extent do you believe in Jesus based on what others have told you (vs. 42)? To what extent do you believe based on first-hand experience?

9. What questions were probably going through the disciples' minds when they listened to Jesus in verses 32 through 38? (What food? What work? Why four months? What fields? What harvest? What's this guy talking about?)

10. Later, when Jesus returned to Cana, the key to the healing of the official's son (vss. 43-54) was the same as the conversion of the woman at the well—"The man took Jesus at his word" (vs. 50). How does this story apply to your life? (We know, intellectually, a lot of things Jesus has promised us. But we then need to have the faith to truly believe that Jesus will do those things for us.)

SO WHAT?

Hand out copies of the reproducible sheet, "Thirst Quenchers," to each group member. Have them write down or discuss what the individuals might be thirsty for, and some things they could say to these people to bring Jesus into the conversation. Pray for sensitivity to people's real needs and opportunities to talk with them about Jesus.

THIRST QUENCHERS

Like the woman at the well, all people are thirsty. For each person listed, what might he/she be thirsty for, and what are some things you could say, or questions you could ask, to get him or her thinking about Jesus?

What this person might be thirsty for

What you could say to or ask this person

A friend whose brother just died of AIDS.

A new kid at school who seems really lonely.

A guy who's an excellent athlete, but seems obsessed with his body.

A girl who has a real drinking problem.

A classmate who's into reincarnation and stuff like that.

A friend who's sleeping around.

JOHN 5

A Pool Party and a Sabbath Sermon

As Jesus is traveling, He comes upon a man by the Bethesda pool who has been an invalid for 38 years. The good news is that Jesus heals the man and tells him, "Pick up your mat and walk." The bad news is that this happens on the Sabbath, and the Jewish leaders say that carrying a mat is improper "work" on a holy day. This leads to a detailed discourse by Jesus, justifying His authority and challenging that of the religious establishment.

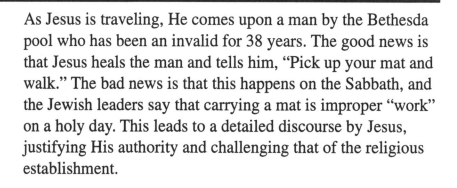

The reproducible sheet, "Worst-Case Scenario," will help group members contemplate some of the least pleasurable experiences that could happen to them. When they finish, have them share some of their responses. Then explain that the first story in John 5 deals with a perennial loser whose worst-case scenario was transformed into something extraordinary by Christ.

DATE I USED THIS SESSION _____ GROUP I USED IT WITH _____

NOTES FOR NEXT TIME _____

_____

_____

1. When was the last time you wanted something really badly, but couldn't get it because you weren't fast enough, strong enough, rich enough, etc.? (Examples: Sports honors; membership in some organization; radio promotions to "call and get two free tickets", etc.)

2. When you want something a lot, how long do you usually pursue it before you give up? (This will depend on the desired item. Some goals are lifelong. Others we outgrow, lose interest in, or just give up on.)

3. If you were the person described in verses 1-7, how do you think you would feel? Why? (Explain that the man was by the pool because the water was believed to have some sort of healing power—if he could be the first person in after the water was stirred. Unfortunately, he never got there first.) How many years would you have waited before giving up?

4. Why do you think Jesus asked, "Do you want to get well?" (vs. 6)? Isn't that pretty obvious? Explain. (Perhaps the man had given up all hope of getting well. Maybe he had gotten used to his condition and didn't really want to change. Perhaps Jesus was simply giving him an opportunity to express his faith.)

5. Do you know people who seem to enjoy other people's suffering, and resent other people's success? What do you think motivates people to respond the way the religious leaders did in verses 8-10? (Jealousy, legalism, etc.)

6. Beyond taking care of his problem, what did Jesus do for this guy that He will also do for us (vss. 11-15)? (He followed up with him after he had encountered opposition, showing that He was concerned about his spiritual, as well as physical, well-being. Jesus does not save us and then leave us on our own. Nor should we receive His forgiveness and then forget about Him. The relationship should be ongoing.)

7. When Jesus began to explain that His authority to save and to heal—even on the Sabbath—reflected His direct relationship with God the Father, He faced fierce opposition from the Jewish authorities (vss. 16-18). He listed a

number of similarities between Himself and His Father. What did He list? (Doing the same things [vs. 19], giving life [vs. 21], the right to judge [vss. 22-40], receive honor [vs. 23], etc.) **Of course, anyone could *say* these things, so how did Jesus back up what He was saying** (vss. 31-47)? (He referred His opponents to the testimony of John the Baptist, the work that He [Jesus] was doing which could only be accomplished by God, and the Old Testament Scriptures. Yet He realized that lack of faith would prevent people from believing any of these things.)

8. **On a scale of 1 (least) to 10 (most), how much do you think you would have believed in Jesus at this point in His ministry if you had been living during this time?**

9. **These Jewish leaders claimed to believe the Scriptures, but when they were fulfilled before their eyes in the form of the promised Messiah, they weren't willing to believe** (vss. 41-47). **Are you like them at all? For instance, how would you complete the following sentences: (a) I believe in Jesus, but I don't think He . . . ; (b) I believe in the Bible, but . . . ; (c) I think God loves me, but . . .** (If group members don't express any current doubts, have them discuss doubts of their pasts, or of their friends.)

(Needed: File cards and pens)

Explain that we, like the religious leaders in this chapter, may know Bible verses without really knowing God. We need to read the Word of God in order to get to know the God of the Word. As someone has said, reading the Bible without focusing on the Lord is as absurd as reading a road map of Colorado and saying you've seen the Rockies. Encourage your group to remember that Christianity isn't just about rituals or rules: it's about relating with a real Person. Pass out file cards and have kids finish this sentence: "Christianity without Christ is like . . ." On the back of the card, have them write down some things they can do this week to strengthen their relationship with Jesus.

WORST CASE SCENARIO

Life is filled with wonderfully joyful and pleasant experiences. And then there are the other kind. Answer the following questions, and determine what things would truly be "the worst that could happen" to you.

1. If I were at a formal party where I had to eat what I was served (or seriously offend the host), the thing I would most hate to be served is:

_____ Tofu surprise
_____ Sushi
_____ Steak Tartare (Raw meat, for you non-connoisseurs)
_____ Crunchy fried insect assortment
_____ Other:

2. If I were on my first date with someone, the worst thing that could happen would be if I:

_____ Had the world's largest zit on my nose
_____ Got a phone call from my mother in the middle of dinner
_____ Called my date the wrong name
_____ Noticed the other person yawning whenever I talked
_____ Other:

3. If my father or mother got a big raise and promotion, but had to transfer somewhere else as part of the package, the worst place to go would be:

_____ Deep in the jungles of the Amazon
_____ Stationed on a ship that doesn't dock for months at a time
_____ A desert outpost
_____ The town of:
_____ Other:

4. If I were in a tragic accident and were seriously injured, I would most hate to lose:

_____ My vision
_____ My hearing
_____ My ability to speak
_____ My ability to walk
_____ Other:

5. The worst thing I can imagine happening is:

_____ The death of a family member or close friend
_____ Nuclear war within the boundaries of our country
_____ Receiving a 10-year jail sentence for something I didn't do
_____ Flunking out of school and having a minimum-wage job the rest of my life
_____ Other:

6. The worst thing a person can do to himself or herself is:

_____ Refuse to take risks and live up to his or her full potential
_____ Use drugs
_____ Suffer abuse from someone else without telling anyone
_____ Commit suicide
_____ Other:

JOHN 6

Jesus Makes Dinner; Some Disciples Desert

Jesus' words and actions force people to make hard decisions about Him. First, His miraculous ability to feed the crowd of over 5,000 causes some people to want to make Him king. His walking on water displays further power. But in spite of these things, some of His followers can't understand His teachings about being the Bread of Life, and they reject Him.

(Needed: A loaf of bread for each team)

Divide into teams and give one person on each team a loaf of bread. The other members of his or her team should be some distance across the room. On your signal, the goal of each person is to "feed" his team by tossing pieces of bread into their mouths. They may not use their hands to catch the bread. The first bread tosser to get a piece (or two, or three) into each person's mouth wins. Later, explain that as impressive as this feat was, Jesus' feeding of over 5,000 was far more incredible.

DATE I USED THIS SESSION _____ GROUP I USED IT WITH _____

NOTES FOR NEXT TIME_____

_____

_____

1. What's the most memorable picnic you've ever been on? What things make it stand out in your mind: The food? The beauty of the day? The fun you had with friends? (Explain that the outing where Jesus fed 5,000 people with five small loaves and two small fish was probably very memorable to those people.)

2. How would you have answered Jesus' "test" question (vss. 5, 6)? (What exactly was Jesus testing for? What answer do you suppose He was hoping to hear?)

3. When Jesus posed the problem to His disciples of feeding the crowd, He received two responses. Are you more like Philip (vss. 5-7), or Andrew (vss. 8, 9)? Why? (Philip immediately translated the problem into financial terms. Andrew knew the problem wasn't a financial one and was willing to face the situation, but was convinced that he would be unable to.)

4. What do you think is important about verse 11? (Besides giving thanks for the food, it's significant to see that all the people received as much as they wanted to eat. Jesus fully satisfies our needs. It's a physical need here, but later in the chapter, He makes a spiritual connection [vss. 27, 35].)

5. Why do you think Jesus didn't want anything to be wasted (vss. 12, 13)? Couldn't He do the same thing the next time He wanted to eat? (Miracles of God should never be taken for granted. Good stewardship of God's provisions is just as important as receiving them to begin with.)

6. How did the people respond to Jesus' miracle (vss. 14, 15)? (They would have made Him king if He had allowed it.) How do you respond as you hear about this miraculous event? (The impact on us should be the same. Anyone capable of such things should be "king" of our lives.)

7. After the feeding of over 5,000, the disciples got 3 1/2 miles out on the lake in the middle of a storm. They saw Jesus walking across the water to join them (vss. 16-24). Their response was terror. Does the power of God ever frighten you? (If not, perhaps we're not looking closely enough.)

8. How well do you feel you do "the work of God" as defined by Jesus (vss. 25-29)? (Group members should determine to what extent they believe in Jesus [vs. 29].)

9. Just as the Israelites received manna in the desert to keep them alive, Jesus explained that He is the "bread of life" sent from heaven (vss. 30-50). Some objected that "the son of Joseph" claimed to be heaven-sent (vss. 41, 42). But what caused even more of an outrage (vss. 48-59)? (When He started speaking in terms of people eating His flesh and drinking His blood, His hearers were shocked and offended. They didn't understand that Jesus spoke symbolically of Himself as a sacrifice for their sins.)

10. If you were one of the people listening to Jesus that day, do you think you would have grumbled [vss. 41, 61], argued [vs. 52], or believed [vs. 69]? Why?

11. Jesus' harder teachings weeded out those who were following Him for the "fun" of it from those who were spiritually prepared to hear what He was teaching (vss. 60-71). What are some of the "hard" teachings of Christianity that keep people from following Jesus today? (Denying oneself; putting Jesus above family and friends; loving enemies, etc.)

The reproducible sheet, "That's a Tough One," asks group members to think through some of Jesus' sayings that might make it difficult for young people to follow Him today. When they finish, work as a group to try to put some of those things into perspective. (You may want to have some good Bible commentaries available.) Studying these statements may make them easier to understand, but they will always be difficult to apply. For every verse listed, try to come up with two promises of God or reasons to give thanks in spite of that difficulty. When our primary focus shifts from the things that are difficult to the love and power of God, our perspective tends to improve.

That's a TOUGH One

Mark Twain once said something like, "It's not the things I don't understand about the Bible that bother me, it's the things I do understand that bother me!" Below are some of the statements Jesus made that might be difficult to understand or, even worse, difficult to follow. Circle the response beside each statement that best describes how you feel.

"If anyone comes to me and does not hate his father and mother, his wife and children, his brothers and sisters—yes, even his own life—he cannot be my disciple." (Luke 14:26; see also Matthew 10:37-39)

NO PROBLEM! | **TOUGH, BUT I CAN HANDLE IT.** | **I UNDERSTAND IT, BUT I DON'T LIKE IT.** | **I DON'T EVEN UNDERSTAND IT.**

"No one who puts his hand to the plow and looks back is fit for service in the kingdom of God." (Luke 9:62)

NO PROBLEM! | **TOUGH, BUT I CAN HANDLE IT.** | **I UNDERSTAND IT, BUT I DON'T LIKE IT.** | **I DON'T EVEN UNDERSTAND IT.**

"If anyone would come after me, he must deny himself and take up his cross daily and follow me. For whoever wants to save his life will lose it, but whoever loses his life for me will save it." (Luke 9:23, 24)

NO PROBLEM! | **TOUGH, BUT I CAN HANDLE IT.** | **I UNDERSTAND IT, BUT I DON'T LIKE IT.** | **I DON'T EVEN UNDERSTAND IT.**

"No one can serve two masters. Either he will hate the one and love the other, or he will be devoted to the one and despise the other. You cannot serve both God and Money." (Matthew 6:24)

NO PROBLEM! | **TOUGH, BUT I CAN HANDLE IT.** | **I UNDERSTAND IT, BUT I DON'T LIKE IT.** | **I DON'T EVEN UNDERSTAND IT.**

"In the same way, any of you who does not give up everything he has cannot be my disciple." (Luke 14:33)

NO PROBLEM! | **TOUGH, BUT I CAN HANDLE IT.** | **I UNDERSTAND IT, BUT I DON'T LIKE IT.** | **I DON'T EVEN UNDERSTAND IT.**

"I am the way and the truth and the life. No one comes to the Father except through me." (John 14:6)

NO PROBLEM! | **TOUGH, BUT I CAN HANDLE IT.** | **I UNDERSTAND IT, BUT I DON'T LIKE IT.** | **I DON'T EVEN UNDERSTAND IT.**

JOHN 7

The Christ Controversy: Part 1

CHAPTER CHECK

After having performed a number of miracles, Jesus teaches some difficult concepts about Himself. As a result, the people's opinions about Him become greatly divided. Is He a good man? A deceiver? A new prophet? Demon possessed? Or could He possibly be the Christ? And while Jesus still maintains a low profile, He continues to teach and to respond to people's questions.

OPENING ACT

(Needed: Two buckets, water, large chunk of ice)

Before meeting, make a large chunk of ice; keep it hidden from your group. Then fill a bucket with water and place an empty bucket a few yards away. Present the following challenge to your group: **I bet I can carry more water in one hand than four of you can carry in one hand combined.** Let groups of four see how much water they can scoop into one hand from one bucket and carry to the other one. Measure the quantity of each group's combined attempt. When it's your turn, bring out your large chunk of ice and carry it in one hand to the other bucket. Kids will no doubt object, but tell them ice is simply frozen water. Use this exercise to lead into a discussion of how Jesus' brothers didn't believe Him either.

DATE I USED THIS SESSION _____ GROUP I USED IT WITH _____

NOTES FOR NEXT TIME _____

_____

_____

1. Has anybody close to you ever doubted your abilities or held you back in any way? If so, how did it make you feel? Why do people sometimes hold back or put down the abilities of those they are close to?

2. What do you think Jesus' brothers (or half-brothers, to be more accurate) really thought about Him (vss. 1-5)? (They seemed to encourage Him, though they didn't truly believe in Him. It seems that they wanted to see what others thought before they made up their own minds.)

3. How would you describe Jesus' popularity at this time? (Mixed. Lots of people were talking about Him privately [vs. 12], but few seemed to really understand who He was. The Jewish leaders did not endorse the actions of Jesus, so people were afraid to talk about Jesus publicly [vs. 13].)

4. Why do you think Jesus' teaching sounded so different from that of the Jewish leaders (vss. 14-24)? (Jesus spoke with the authority of God. The others based their rules on the laws of Moses. And while the Old Testament law was certainly valid, it had been shrouded in hundreds of years' worth of tradition and interpretation. People were losing sight of the original intent of the law.)

5. What kept a lot of people from believing that Jesus was the Christ (vss. 25-31)? (He didn't meet their expectations for "the Christ." The Messiah was prophesied to be from Bethlehem [Judea], not Nazareth [Galilee]. They thought they knew all about Jesus as a person, but they didn't, so they didn't recognize Him as God.) **How do you think people might do the same things today?**

6. Jesus knew exactly what would happen to Him, and He thoroughly confused the Jewish leaders with this information (vss. 32-36). **But do you think there were any drawbacks for Him knowing His future?** (Everything Jesus did was with the full knowledge that He would soon die. In light of such knowledge, His love and forgiveness should seem even more incredible.)

7. Did Jesus try to tone down His message a bit when He knew others were looking to have Him arrested (vss. 35-39)? Explain. How does His example apply to us? (Jesus knew His future was in the hands of God, so He continued to speak boldly. So should we.)

8. The debate in verses 45 through 52 took place behind closed doors among the religious leaders. But Jesus had at least one ally there. Who was he, and why was he so supportive? (Nicodemus didn't want the others to act too hastily because he had made the effort to talk to Jesus personally [John 3:1-21]. The closer we get to Jesus, the better we understand His teachings.)

9. Go through the entire chapter and make a list of all the different views people had about who Jesus was. (A good man [vs. 12], a deceiver [vs. 12], demon-posessed [vs. 20], a prophet [vs. 40], the Christ [vs. 41].) **Why was the opinion so divided? Who do people today think Jesus is? Who do you say He is?**

The reproducible sheet, "Off the Fence," will help your group members determine where they are in regard to their relationships with Jesus. As they share answers with the rest of the group, see how often they feel they are in the minority, as opposed to when they go along with the crowd. Discuss: **How is Jesus unlike any person who ever lived?** (He's the only sinless person, the only one who helped create the world, the only one who can forgive sins, etc.) **If Jesus appeared in person today and performed a great miracle, do you think everyone would believe that He is truly the Son of God? Why or why not?**

OFF THE FENCE

When Jesus came to earth, people had all kinds of opinions about who He was. And now, a couple of thousand years later, things are not much different. Some feel that Jesus was nobody special. Some insist that He was definitely the Son of God. Others try to "ride the fence" about many of the issues concerning Him. As you can see, we've started you "on the fence" with several such issues below. What you need to do is:

(1) Position yourself to the right or left of the fence to show how strongly you agree with each statement. (Far left = Totally Disagree; Far right = Totally Agree)

(2) For each issue, estimate what percentage of people your age would be to the left of the fence, to the right of the fence, and riding the fence.

Disagree						Agree				
5 4 3 2 1					There is only one God in the form of God the Father, Jesus the Son, and the Holy Spirit.	1 2 3 4 5				
5 4 3 2 1					Jesus has the power to perform miracles.	1 2 3 4 5				
5 4 3 2 1					Jesus was just a good man—like Buddha, Muhammad, and other religious people.	1 2 3 4 5				
5 4 3 2 1					I am willing to do anything Jesus asks—no matter how embarrassing or difficult I think it might be.	1 2 3 4 5				
5 4 3 2 1					I am working hard to be ready when Jesus returns.	1 2 3 4 5				
5 4 3 2 1					I boldly express my opinion when Jesus is not being fairly spoken about.	1 2 3 4 5				
5 4 3 2 1					I am willing to endure the comments of others who reject my commitment to Christianity.	1 2 3 4 5				
5 4 3 2 1					Jesus never really lived, or if He did, He didn't rise from the dead.	1 2 3 4 5				
5 4 3 2 1					Rejecting Jesus' offer of salvation leads to judgment and hell.	1 2 3 4 5				

JOHN 8

The Christ Controversy: Part 2

CHAPTER CHECK

A woman caught in the act of adultery is brought before Jesus by religious officials eager to stone her, and He teaches them an embarrassing lesson on forgiveness. After asserting that He is the Light of the World, Jesus talks with the Pharisees about His right to speak for God. He explains His identity in relation to the Father and the Jewish forefathers.

OPENING ACT

Hand out the reproducible sheet, "Caught in the Act," and let students complete it. Then let them discuss how they made their decisions. See which group members were more "forgiving" and which ones were "hanging judges." Hold a "mock trial" for any situation where opinion is strongly divided—first hearing arguments from the prosecution, and then from the defense. Discuss the differences between justice, mercy, and grace as you approach the story of the woman caught in adultery.

DATE I USED THIS SESSION _____ GROUP I USED IT WITH _____

NOTES FOR NEXT TIME _____

_____

_____

1. Have you ever gotten "off the hook" for a punishment you deserved? What were the circumstances and how did you feel?

2. Imagine the setting as this chapter opens. It's dawn. You've gone down to the temple to hear Jesus tell you more about God. Suddenly the religious leaders haul in a woman who has just been caught in bed with someone else's husband. They stand her up in front of everyone and ask Jesus what to do. How would you feel as a spectator? If you were the woman? If you were Jesus?

3. Why do you suppose they caught the woman, but not the man (vss. 1-6)? (They simply viewed her as a "pawn" in their scheme to trap Jesus. Women, especially promiscuous ones, were degraded in society's eyes.)

4. Based on Jesus' response (vss. 7, 8), do you think He was suggesting that we should be able to get away with sin because no one is worthy of passing judgment on us? **Explain.** (No. We are all accountable for our wrongdoings, but God is the one who ultimately judges us, or forgives us. Jesus merely prevented the Pharisees from short-circuiting God's forgiveness of this woman.)

5. Do you think Jesus let the woman off lightly (vss. 9-11)? (Though it may seem so, we must remember that this woman was just saved from dying. In that context, Jesus' command to "leave your life of sin" is more than a flippant remark. His expression of freedom carried with it a sense of responsibility.)

6. In what ways is Jesus the "light of the world" (vs. 12)? (He exposes the darkness of our sin [searchlight], He shows us how to live [spotlight], He brings hope [lighthouse], He gives life [sunlight], etc.)

7. As Jesus tried to explain who He really was, the Jewish leaders wanted a second witness to back up what He was saying (vss. 12-30). **Who did Jesus cite as His other witness, and what confusion did that cause?** (When Jesus said that His Father would back Him up, the Pharisees wanted to know where His father was—revealing that they couldn't [or wouldn't] understand what He was saying.)

8. **Even the people who believed in Jesus found it hard to understand what He was trying to tell them** (vss. 31-47). **In what ways do you think we tend to be like those people?** (Sometimes we believe we are free of outside influences on us; yet we are still trapped in some sin that we haven't yet identified or mastered. Jesus challenges us to face the truth and become completely free.)

9. **Some of Jesus' statements were so radical that many of the people assumed He must be demon-possessed** (vss. 48, 52). **What was the final issue that caused a lot of those present to reject Jesus' statements outright** (vss. 48-59), **and what was their response?** (When Jesus claimed that He existed before Abraham, the crowd was ready to stone Him.)

10. **Why do you think Jesus didn't speak more plainly about His identity?** (Perhaps if He had spoken clearly, the religious leaders would have arrested Him too soon. Even as it was, they were ready to stone Him in verse 59.)

11. **How do you respond when you strongly disagree with someone, or when you're in a conversation you just can't follow and you feel "stupid"?** (Withdraw; get violent; raise your voice to keep up a good front, etc. Explain that this is the position the Pharisees found themselves in as they debated with Jesus.)

(Needed: Videotaping equipment [optional])

If possible, get a video camera and record a series of "man on the street" interviews in which kids ask one on-the-spot question of people at school, at work, at the local shopping mall: "Who do you think Jesus of Nazareth was?" You could then show this at a future meeting and discuss it. If this isn't possible, consider asking the same question in a simple phone survey. Then read John 8:31-38. Have kids ponder questions like the following: **Do you know the truth? Have you been set free? Are you a son or a slave?**

CAUGHT IN THE ACT

For each of the following, decide how forgiving you would be. Circle the check mark to show where your decision lies between the two options.

(1) An A-student panics when, on just one test, he isn't prepared and tries to cheat. He gets caught, and the usual punishment is a two-day out-of-school suspension. What do you think should happen?

Give him a break! ✓ ✓ ✓ ✓ ✓ ✓ ✓ ✓ ✓ ✓ ✓ ✓ ✓ ✓ ✓ ✓ ✓ **Slam him!**

(2) Cassandra Smith has a huge party at her house on a weekend when her parents are out of town— without their permission. The house gets trashed: the coffee table gets scratched up pretty badly, a window gets broken, someone throws up all over the living room couch, and someone drops pizza facedown onto the Smiths' brand-new non-stain-resistant carpet. When Cassandra's parents get home, they hit the roof. What should they do?

Give her a break! ✓ ✓ ✓ ✓ ✓ ✓ ✓ ✓ ✓ ✓ ✓ ✓ ✓ ✓ ✓ ✓ **Slam her!**

(3) Bob breaks up with Jane after dating for two years because Alice has been paying a lot of attention to him. Three weeks later, Alice is paying attention to Jason, and Bob wants Jane back. What should Jane do?

Give him a break! ✓ ✓ ✓ ✓ ✓ ✓ ✓ ✓ ✓ ✓ ✓ ✓ ✓ ✓ ✓ ✓ ✓ **Slam him!**

(4) James' friend, Allison, gets pregnant and drops out of school and church activities for several months to have the baby. During her absence, rumors begin to fly about who the father is—some say it's James (it's not). When Allison comes back, people make fun of her and say they think James is the father. Allison doesn't deny it. One day, Allison calls James up and asks a favor of him. What should James do?

Give her a break! ✓ ✓ ✓ ✓ ✓ ✓ ✓ ✓ ✓ ✓ ✓ ✓ ✓ ✓ ✓ ✓ **Slam her!**

(5) Steve and some of his friends go out to celebrate their big win on Friday night. They have a few drinks, even though they're underage. A police officer pulls them over, and Steve admits they had a few beers to celebrate their victory, but that they aren't drunk. What should the police officer do?

Give 'em a break! ✓ ✓ ✓ ✓ ✓ ✓ ✓ ✓ ✓ ✓ ✓ ✓ ✓ ✓ ✓ ✓ **Slam 'em!**

JOHN 9

Blind Man's Bluff?

Jesus' healing of a blind man causes quite a stir among the man's friends and the Pharisees. Some couldn't accept the fact that the man had been healed. Others questioned the authority of Jesus to heal the man. The man's parents were dragged into the debate. Eventually the man was thrown out of the synagogue, though he found something far better.

(Needed: Blindfold, an assortment of foods, and a grocery bag)

Before meeting, place an assortment of at least ten different foods (peas, chocolate candies, peanuts, popcorn, potatoes, carrots, chewing gum, banana, pretzels, lettuce, etc.) in a bag. Blindfold group members one at a time and let them feel things in the bag for thirty seconds. (If your group is large, have more than one bag with identical items, so people can take turns at the same time.) After feeling, have them write down everything they felt. Award a prize (something from the bag that's wrapped) to the person who identifies the most items. This exercise might help group members be more sympathetic as they study the plight of the blind man in this chapter.

DATE I USED THIS SESSION _____ GROUP I USED IT WITH _____

NOTES FOR NEXT TIME _____

_____

_____

1. Can you think of anything you really wanted, but once you got it, it caused problems you hadn't foreseen? (Perhaps a date that didn't work out; a "new" used car that, upon purchase, rapidly fell apart; the latest CD by a new artist that had only one good song on it; etc.)

2. The blind man in this chapter was singled out because of a belief during this time that suffering (such as blindness) must be caused by sin. If the man himself hadn't sinned, it was thought, his parents might have done something terrible for which he was being punished. But Jesus added a third option that could explain the man's blindness (vss. 1-5). **What was it?** (In this case, the man's blindness was a means for Jesus to display the power of God.)

3. Jesus healed the blind man (vss. 6, 7). **What conflict did this cause between the once-blind man and the people who thought they knew him** (vss. 8-12)? (The man's friends wanted him to prove that he had been healed by describing how the miracle had taken place, which, of course, he could only explain up to a point.)

4. And since the healing had taken place on the Sabbath (vs. 14), **the Pharisees wanted to investigate. What conflict arose among them** (vss. 13-16)? (Based on their interpretation of Mosaic law, some believed Jesus could not be sent from God. Others couldn't dispute the power He displayed.)

5. The Pharisees weren't willing to believe the man's testimony that he had been blind since birth, so they sent for his parents. And the man's parents seemed to "plead the fifth amendment." **Why** (vss. 17-23)? (They were afraid of being kicked out of the synagogue—and becoming social and spiritual "outcasts" among the Jews—which had been threatened for anyone who stated a belief that Jesus was the Christ.)

6. When investigating the parents didn't work out, the Pharisees called the man back. They were obviously trying to sway his opinions about Jesus, but his response to them is a classic one (vss. 24, 25). **What can we learn from his example?** (We won't always know all the answers to the

137

questions we are asked about Jesus; yet we can testify to what He has done for *us*. People can argue with theology, but they can't argue with biography.)

7. **But then the Pharisees pushed a little too hard and the debate between themselves and the man got a more heated** (vss. 26-34). **Do you think anything the man said was out of line? Do you think he deserved the sentence he received? Explain.** (Point out that the man could easily have made a general statement that would have appeased the Pharisees. Yet his faith had already begun to solidify in regard to Jesus. He was getting bolder.)

8. **When Jesus sought out the man to talk to him** (vss. 35-38), **why do you think the guy wasn't any more bitter about having lost his status in the synagogue?** (He had found something better. He had not only received his sight, but he had also found a Savior.)

9. **In what ways were the Pharisees and the blind man similar? How were they different?** (Both were "blind" in a sense. The man's physical blindness was apparent, and he was eager to do something to remedy it. The Pharisees weren't willing to admit their spiritual blindness. As long as the blind Pharisees claimed to be able to see, they would not feel the need for Jesus to do anything about it.)

10. **In what ways are people still "blind" to Jesus today?** (Some refuse to "see" their own sinful state; some refuse to see His one-of-a-kind saving power, etc.)

This chapter deals with a variety of responses to Jesus from a rather diverse mix of people. Hand out the reproducible sheet, "Yearbook—Yourbook" and give your students time to think about some contemporary "stereotypes" of followers of Christ. Do any of these stereotypes have some basis in reality? They can then complete their "self-portraits." As time permits, give those who are interested a chance to discuss their drawings.

Check out this yearbook full of Christian "stereotypes" and then draw one of your own in the

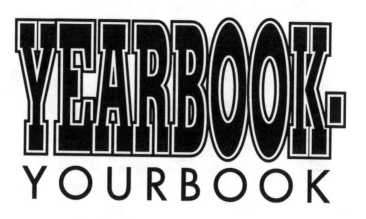
YEARBOOK. YOURBOOK

center that you feel describes yourself as a Christian at this point in your life.

Brad Attitude
Nickname: THE REBEL
Slogan: You got a problem with that?

Joy B. Gone
Nickname: THE COMPLAINER
Slogan: Woe is me!

John "Hippo" Krit
Nickname: THE CHAMELEON
Slogan: When in Rome, do as the Romans do.

Ivana Bea Faux
Nickname: THE MANNEQUIN
Slogan: Never let them see you sweat—or cry.

Your name:
Nickname:
Slogan:

Holly Roller
Nickname: RIGHTEOUS RAIDER
Slogan: Believe it—or else.

S. Marty Pants
Nickname: THE CRITIC
Slogan: You're wrong.

Guy Nextdoor
Nickname: NICE & EASY
Slogan: Don't rock the boat.

Leo N. Ranger
Nickname: CLOSET CHRISTIAN
Slogan: On my own again.

Sheep Crossing

As Jesus teaches, He presents Himself as the Gate for the sheep and the Good Shepherd whose main concern is for the sheep. In contrast are the "hired hands" who oversee the sheep, but for their own rewards. Such teaching angers certain Jewish leaders to the point of trying to kill Him, but Jesus escapes them. In the meantime, many put their faith in Him.

(Needed: Blindfold)

Have group members stand in a circle with arms reaching in toward the center of the circle. Put a blindfolded volunteer in the middle. Spin the volunteer around several times and have him or her walk until bumping in to someone's hand. The volunteer should try to guess who this person is by saying, "Say 'baa.'" The person who was touched should say, "baa" in a disguised voice. This exchange can take place three times before the volunteer must make a guess. If correct, he/she gets to sit down, and the identified person goes to the center. If wrong, the volunteer should try again. Switch volunteers after three unsuccessful attempts. This activity will remind kids of the need to recognize Jesus' voice.

DATE I USED THIS SESSION _____ GROUP I USED IT WITH _____

NOTES FOR NEXT TIME _____

_____

_____

1. Have you ever been misled by a "wolf in sheep's clothing"—someone who appeared to be friendly and innocent, yet who was simply deceiving you for his or her own benefit? If so, describe what happened and how you felt.

2. In what sense is Jesus a "gate" (vss. 1-10)? (It's only through Him that we can find eternal life.)

3. How do the sheep tell one person from another (vss. 3-5)? (They listen for the voice that is familiar to them. If they recognize it, they follow. If not, they run.)

4. As Jesus discussed these basic truths with His listeners, they had no idea what He was talking about (vs. 6). So He identified Himself as the Good Shepherd (vss. 11, 14). In what ways is He like a shepherd? (He guides us. He cares for us—even to the point of laying down His life for us.) Who do you think He had in mind as the "thieves and robbers" (vss. 7-10)? (The Pharisees and religious leaders had set themselves up as overseers to God's people, but most of them were self-centered and in it for their own good.) What are some examples of people using religion to further their own self-interests today?

5. According to verse 10, what does Jesus have in mind for you as one of His sheep? How do you think this promise might specifically apply to us? (Jesus came to provide us with "abundant life," or "life to the full." Have group members suggest what this might mean to them.)

6. What is the major difference between the Good Shepherd and someone merely hired to oversee the sheep (vss. 11-13)? (A hired hand runs away when danger threatens because he has no real concern for the sheep, but a good shepherd is willing to lay down his life for the sheep.)

7. Jesus spoke of other sheep He had who were not in this same sheep pen (vss. 14-16). Who do you think He was referring to, and why is this a significant statement? (Jesus came to redeem the sins of the world—not just those of the Jewish people.)

8. So far, Jesus' listeners had been confused, but attentive. But what did He say that agitated them and caused them to be divided (vss. 17-21)? (Jesus spoke of God as His Father. He also said that He would voluntarily die and come back to life again.)

9. Still, the Jewish listeners weren't convinced that Jesus was stating that He was the Christ who had been prophesied, so a little later they pressed Him on the issue. What evidence did He offer to convince them (vss. 22-30)? (He told them plainly; He performed miracles; many people had already responded to Him; and He was one with God the Father.)

10. After His bold statements, what kind of response did Jesus get from most of the religious leaders (vss. 31-39)? (They wanted to stone Him on the spot, or at least arrest Him.)

11. But when Jesus withdrew to a place away from the hostility of the religious leaders, how was He received (vss. 40-42)? (The people saw that He was exactly the person John the Baptist had prophesied, and many believed in Him.)

12. This chapter contains several questions about Jesus (vss. 19, 21, 24). **If you were around at this time, what questions would you have been asking?**

SO WHAT?

The imagery of Jesus as the Good Shepherd is carried on in the reproducible sheet, "You Are Getting Sheepy." Students are asked to identify what kind of sheep they are. Share responses as appropriate. Then brainstorm a list of "Ways to Be Better Sheep." Answers should reflect sheep-like tendencies rather than human ones: "Don't stray too far away to hear the shepherd's voice," "Stay away from wolves," etc. But in learning to be better sheep, you are almost certain to learn to be better Christians as well.

You Are Getting SHEEPY

Take this quiz to see what kind of a sheep you are.

1 Which of these famous sheep best describes you?
( ) Mary's little lamb (whose fleece was white as snow)
( ) The one sheep out of a hundred who gets lost in Luke 15:3-7
( ) Other:

2 Are you . . .
( ) happily inside the sheepfold?
( ) inside the fold, but climbing the walls to get out?
( ) outside the sheepfold wanting to get in?
( ) happily outside the sheepfold?
( ) not sure

3 Where are you in relation to the Shepherd?
( ) Very close
( ) Not as close as I'd like, but getting closer
( ) I keep my distance
( ) What Shepherd?

4 Concerning wolves, do you . . .
( ) run whenever you see one?
( ) hang around with them, because they aren't really so bad?
( ) what wolves?

5 How good are you at hearing the Shepherd's voice?
( ) It's music to my ears
( ) Sometimes other voices make it hard to hear
( ) Eh?

6 What's the best thing about being a sheep?
_____
_____
_____
_____
_____

7 What's the hardest thing about being a sheep?
_____
_____
_____
_____
_____

That About Wraps It Up

After hearing that His good friend Lazarus is seriously ill, Jesus appears to dawdle before going to Bethany. When He gets there, Lazarus has been dead for four days. Yet all along, Jesus assures everyone that Lazarus will be OK. After claiming to be "the Resurrection and the Life," Jesus resurrects Lazarus, after which they both become targets that the Pharisees plot to kill.

(Needed: A roll of toilet paper for each team)

Form teams of four or five members each. Give each team a roll or two of toilet paper and the assignment to transform one of its members into a "mummy." You may want to have teams work in close proximity to each other so all the mummies can be seen when the wrapping is completed. If you wish, you can award a prize to the team that does the best job. Later, refer to your mummies as you see how many people would be eager to obey Jesus' command to "Take off the grave clothes and let him go," after the person had been dead for four days.

DATE I USED THIS SESSION _____ GROUP I USED IT WITH _____

NOTES FOR NEXT TIME _____

_____

_____

1. Describe a time when you were really, really sad. What were the circumstances? How do you respond (outwardly) when you're sad inside?

2. Jesus received some news that should have made Him sad (vss. 1-4), yet He didn't seem to be. What was the news, and why didn't Jesus seem to react to it? (Jesus knew exactly what was happening in Bethany, and He knew what would come of it.)

3. With a good friend sick, and other friends worried and upset (vss. 5, 6), why do you think Jesus waited two days before going to Bethany? (He knew Lazarus was already dead, and He was going to display God's power to an unprecedented degree.)

4. The disciples had a different reason for not showing sadness for Lazarus's death. What was it (vss. 7-16)? (They knew Jesus [and consequently, themselves] faced danger in Judea. They seemed more concerned about their own safety than in what Jesus had told them about Lazarus. But also note that Thomas, who so often gets singled out for his lack of faith, is the one in this passage willing to die for Jesus.)

5. When Jesus got to Bethany, He was confronted first by Martha (vss. 17-27) and then Mary (vss. 28-32). What do you think about the faith of these two women? (Both seemed to have quite a bit of faith in Jesus. Among other things, they believed: that Jesus could have saved Lazarus if He had been there [vss. 21, 32]; that Jesus was the Son of God [vs. 27]; and that God would resurrect everyone someday [vs. 24].) How would you say your faith stacks up to theirs?

6. Even though Mary and Martha seemed to understand how special Jesus was, what limitations did they put on His power? (They both believed that He could have done something if He had been physically present and if Lazarus hadn't already died, but they were now at the weeping/mourning stage, beyond any apparent signs of hope [though Martha's statement in verse 22 seems to suggest traces of remaining hope].)

7. Jesus had not previously mourned Lazarus. After all, He knew what He was about to do. So why do you think He wept at this point (vss. 33-37)? (Some say He was moved by the sadness of Mary and Martha [vs. 33]. Others suggest that Jesus felt sad to have to bring Lazarus back from a better place in order to demonstrate the power of God to resurrect the dead. Another view is that He was weeping over the reality and pain of death.)

8. If you had been on hand during the events described in verses 38-44, do you think you could have dared to believe that Lazarus would come walking out of that tomb? Why? What do you think you would have done when he did come out?

9. There were two major responses to Jesus' resurrection of Lazarus. What were they (vss. 45-53)? (Many put their faith in Jesus. Others were threatened by the power that Jesus had, and they plotted to kill Him. [You might also want to jump ahead to the next chapter and point out that Lazarus became an assassination target as well [John 12:9-11.])

10. Do you think Jesus knew what effect such a powerful and public miracle would have on His ministry (vss. 54-57)? (It seems so. He immediately withdrew from the crowds. The next time He appears is during His triumphal entry into Jerusalem, just days before His own death and resurrection [John 12]. It's hard to imagine a more effective display of God's power than raising someone from the dead; yet some still refused to believe.)

The reproducible sheet, "Day of the Living Dead," will have students consider how Lazarus's life might have changed after coming back to life. When they finish, have them carry on the comparison to themselves. If indeed, "we died to sin," (Romans 6:2) then we, too, should have different priorities than we did before "dying." Ask group members to go back through the categories on the sheet and make the same comparisons in their "Before Knowing Jesus" and "After Knowing Jesus" lives. If the differences are insignificant, perhaps more changes should be made in the students' lives.

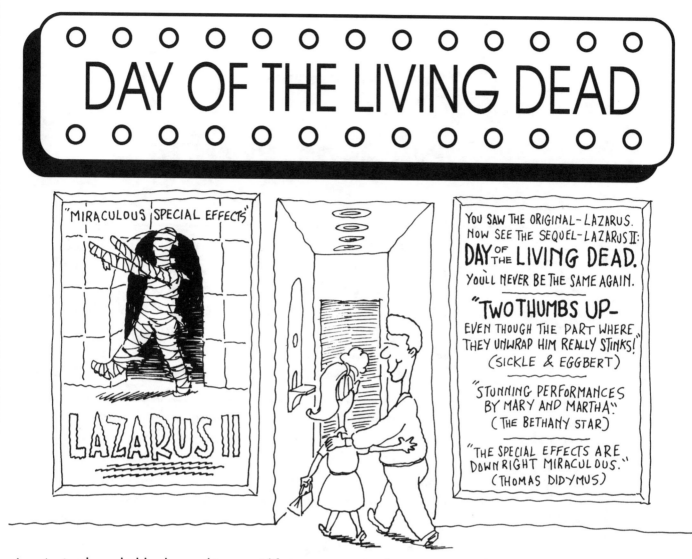

Jesus' miracle probably changed Lazarus' life in many ways. If you were to make two movies about his life, describe the scenes you would include to reflect each of the following areas of his life before and after Jesus raised him from the dead.

	Lazarus (before death)	Lazarus II (after he's raised)
"Chit-chat" topics with neighbors		
Being introduced to new people		
His priorities		
His use of time		
Time spent studying Scripture and praying		
His relationships		
His philosophy of life		

JOHN 12

Fragrant Foreshadowing

CHAPTER ✓ CHECK

When Mary uses expensive perfume to anoint Jesus' feet, Judas complains that it is a waste of money. But Jesus defends Mary's priorities. Meanwhile, Lazarus becomes a walking threat to the integrity of the Pharisees, so they try to have him, as well as Jesus, killed. Jesus then rides triumphantly into Jerusalem, but He makes it known that He will soon die. And response to Jesus continues to be sharply divided.

OPENING ACT

(Needed: Samples of perfume/cologne; a list of names of the fragrances; perfume jar full of water)

Prior to the meeting, collect a number of samples of different perfumes and colognes. Take one of the most expensive brands and empty the contents into another container that you can save. Fill the original bottle with water or some other liquid to match the original color. Set the bogus jar aside. Number the rest, and then hand out a list of the names of all the scents. See who can identify the most correctly. After playing the game, bring out the bogus perfume and pour it down the drain or in the garbage. **What do you think of someone pouring $100 per ounce perfume down the drain?** Use this to lead into John 12.

DATE I USED THIS SESSION _____ GROUP I USED IT WITH _____

NOTES FOR NEXT TIME _____

_____

_____

1. What was the most unusual gift you ever received? Why does it stand out from all the others? (It's from someone very special; it's something only that person could appreciate, etc.)

2. The story in verses 1-8 follows immediately after the story of Jesus raising Lazarus from the dead (John 11). So this party in Jesus' honor—with Lazarus hosting—was pretty special. In light of this, what do you think about Mary's act (vss. 1-3)? (It was certainly unusual. But it showed both adoration [because of the value of the gift] and humility [in the way it was presented].)

3. In today's prices, what was the approximate value of the gift (vss. 4-6)?

4. If you had been there, do you think you might have tended to agree with Judas that perhaps that amount of money could have been put to better use (vss. 4, 5)? Explain your answer.

5. Why did Jesus reject Judas's suggestion and defend Mary's action (vss. 6-8)? (Judas's motives were selfish and impure. Mary, on the other hand, seemed to realize that the perfume would be a better tribute to Jesus while He was alive and with her than as a burial spice after He was dead. While Mary may not have known Jesus would soon die, He knew. And He appreciated the gift.)

6. What was one reason the attendance at the party was so good (vss. 9-11)? (Both Jesus and Lazarus attracted crowds—Jesus because of His miracles, and Lazarus because he had been raised from the dead.)

7. Jesus' popularity continued to grow as He traveled into Jerusalem the next day. How did the people show their support for Jesus (vss. 12-15)? (In both words of praise and spontaneous actions. [Palm branches symbolized victory.])

8. What kept everyone from joining in this celebration (vss. 16-19)? (Even though Jesus quoted Scripture that prophesied this very event, the disciples didn't understand what was going on. And the focus on Jesus just irritated the Pharisees even more.)

9. **But even while people were beginning to clamor to meet with Jesus** (vss. 20-22), **He was turning His attention to His forthcoming death** (vss. 23-26). **Summarize what Jesus said in these verses.** (His death would be like a grain of wheat falling to the ground, dying, and thereby bringing to life many new seeds. Christ's followers must also be willing to "lose" their lives in service to Him.)

10. **What sign was given at this point that indicated Jesus knew exactly what He was talking about** (vss. 27-33)? (God spoke from heaven in response to Jesus' request.)

11. **Some people at this time were confused and still didn't put their faith in Jesus** (vss. 34-41). **Others, quite surprisingly, did believe—but kept their faith a secret** (vss. 42, 43). **If you had been around at the time, how do you think you would have responded?**

12. **Why didn't Jesus seem to take it personally when someone rejected or accepted Him** (vss. 44-50)? (He was speaking on behalf of God the Father. Jesus came to make possible the salvation of the entire world. Whether or not we benefit from His sacrifice is up to each individual.)

13. **If Jesus came to earth today, taught the same truths, and performed a number of amazing miracles, what kinds of different responses do you think He would receive?**

Have kids complete the reproducible student sheet, "The Gift That Keeps on Giving." When they finish, discuss: **Jesus told us that where our treasure is, our hearts would be. As you look at where your money's going, what does it tell you about where your heart might be? Do you tend to give God what is left over, or does His "share" come first? What might this church be able to do if money was no problem?** Without laying on a lot of guilt, remind group members that Jesus certainly notices, appreciates, and loves a cheerful giver (II Corinthians 9:7).

THE
GIFT
THAT KEEPS ON
GIVING

Suppose you had saved up everything you make in a year—all the allowances, all the money for odd jobs, all the nickels and dimes you pick up off the street, all the gifts from your aunt Edith—everything. It's yours to do with as you please.

That's the position Mary was in when she had a jar of expensive perfume. It was worth a year's wages. She had one idea of how to "cash it in." Judas had another. Their solutions might be graphed like this:

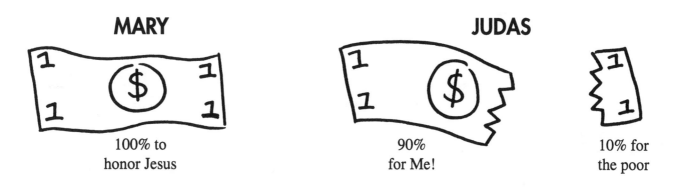

MARY

100% to
honor Jesus

JUDAS

90%
for Me!

10% for
the poor

How would you divvy up a year's worth of cash? The way we use our money depends upon what motivates us: concern for others, saving up for a "rainy day," the high cost of college to come, the "need" for a new car, our own wants, whatever.

Try to divide this dollar bill to illustrate, in proportion, what happens to your money. Divide it into these four categories: spent on necessities, spent on luxuries, saved or invested, and given away.

Upper Room Service

At the Last Supper, Jesus washes His disciples' feet as an example of servanthood. He then predicts His betrayal by Judas and sends him out to make the arrangements for His arrest. Jesus tries to explain to the others what is about to happen, though they don't comprehend. And as soon as Peter pledges his loyalty to the death, Jesus predicts his three-time denial before morning.

(Needed: Washable markers, buckets, soap, water, towels)

Divide into pairs and give each pair a supply of washable markers. Shoes and socks off! Give partners a few minutes to decorate the bottoms of each others' feet. Hold a contest for the most creative designs. Then bring on some buckets of soap and water and wash the ink (as much as you can get at this time) off each others' feet. This should set the stage for the story of Jesus washing the disciples' feet.

DATE I USED THIS SESSION _____ GROUP I USED IT WITH _____

NOTES FOR NEXT TIME_____

_____

_____

1. What is the most sacrificial thing anyone has ever done for you? How did this make you feel about the person making the sacrifice?

2. Jesus had spent the past three years teaching His disciples about the kingdom of God, trying to strengthen their faith and increase their understanding. For the most part, they had been pretty dense. Why do you think Jesus did what He did in verses 1-5, and why was it so surprising? (He wanted to teach them a lesson. Washing feet was considered a servant's job. Knowing His relationship with the Father enabled Jesus to humble Himself in this way.) **How do you think you would have felt at this point?**

3. Peter objected to this at first (vss. 6, 7). **Why do you think he did so?** (While none of the disciples had figured out exactly what was going on with Jesus, Peter did know there was something special about Him. It just didn't seem right to him that Jesus should do something he considered so degrading.)

4. What changed Peter's mind (vss. 8-11)? (Jesus said that such cleansing was an indication of the bond between Himself and His followers. Peter took Him a little too literally, but he certainly wanted to be associated with Jesus in every way.)

5. Why do you think Jesus was making this point at this time in His life? (The concept of willingly giving up His life to die on a cross for humanity was a little too much for most of them to comprehend. But they could understand the humility involved in being willing to wash another's feet.)

6. Examine the scene described in verses 18-30. **What might Jesus have been feeling?** (Sad, disappointed, angry, etc.) **Judas?** (Guilty to have been identified; anxious to get it over with; superior to the others, etc.) **One of the other disciples?** (Confused, uncomfortable, afraid, etc.)

7. Since Jesus would be going away soon, He left the disciples a new commandment that would prove to others that they were associated with Him (vss. 31-35). **What was so new about this commandment?** (It wasn't really new [see

Leviticus 19:18], but Jesus was giving new meaning to what it means to love one another.) **Do you think that commandment is still in effect today? If so, in what ways might we show others that we are Jesus' disciples during the coming week?**

8. Put yourself in Peter's sandals (vss. 36-38). **How do you think he felt after Jesus responded to his pledge of loyalty?**

9. We don't get to see whether Peter or Jesus is correct until John 18 (verses 15-27), **but it's not too hard to guess. Do you think Peter was intentionally lying to Jesus? If not, why do you think he didn't carry through with his promise?** (Most of us tend to be a lot more bold when in a safe setting. From Peter, we should learn not to make rash promises when we don't know what unseen forces or fears we will come up against before we can carry them out.)

Jesus explained that His washing of the disciples' feet was an example they (and we) should imitate (vss. 12-17). But since most of us no longer wear sandals and our roads are not as dirty and dusty, what are some ways we could wash one another's feet today? The reproducible sheet, "Newfangled Foot Washing," will challenge group members to consider suggestions regarding how they might practically "wash others' feet." Fill this sheet out in pairs (perhaps the same pairs you used in the Opening Act). If you want, have pairs pantomime some of their suggestions and have others guess what they're acting out. Then pray for opportunities to serve other people in tangible ways this week.

Newfangled Foot Washing

For each person below, list five specific things you could do to "wash his or her feet." A few examples are given to get you started.

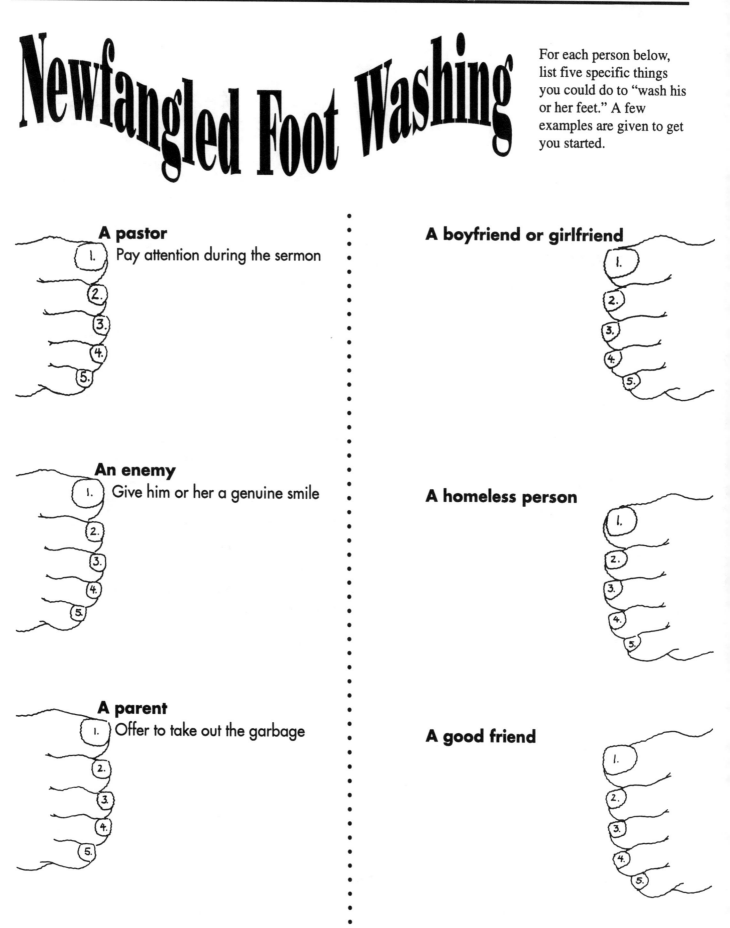

A pastor
1. Pay attention during the sermon
2.
3.
4.
5.

An enemy
1. Give him or her a genuine smile
2.
3.
4.
5.

A parent
1. Offer to take out the garbage
2.
3.
4.
5.

A boyfriend or girlfriend
1.
2.
3.
4.
5.

A homeless person
1.
2.
3.
4.
5.

A good friend
1.
2.
3.
4.
5.

JOHN 14

A Room with a View

As Jesus spends His last hours with the disciples, He tries to prepare them for life without Him. He encourages them to remain faithful, and to relate to the Father as they had related to Him. He promises to go and prepare a place for them and asserts that He's the Way, the Truth, and the Life. After trying to explain Himself yet one more time to His confused disciples, He promises to send the Holy Spirit to help them.

Hand out copies of the reproducible sheet, "Dream Room." Say something like this: **If you had to spend the rest of your life in the same room, what would the room look like?** Let group members design their ideal rooms by drawing in what they'd include and where they'd put it. Tell them they can include anything they want (money's no object), so long as everything fits. Once they finish (or time's up) have volunteers give "tours" of their dream rooms. After several people share their ideas, see if anyone wants to add or change anything about the rooms they created.

DATE I USED THIS SESSION _____ GROUP I USED IT WITH _____

NOTES FOR NEXT TIME _____

_____

_____

1. What room in your house do you like the most and why? What are the attractions of that room? What room in your house do you spend the most time in?

2. Jesus told His disciples He was preparing rooms for them (vss. 1-4). **Do you think that applies to us? If so, what do you think these rooms might be like?** (This passage probably applies to all Jesus' followers.)

3. The good news for His disciples was that Jesus was preparing rooms for them. The bad news was that He was going away. **How did He want them to respond in the meantime?** (He wanted them to trust God as they awaited His eventual return.)

4. As usual, the disciples show that they didn't really understand what Jesus was getting at. First, Thomas asked for directions. **How does Jesus' answer apply to us as well** (vss. 5-7)? (If we truly believe that Jesus is the way, the truth, and the life, we will depend more on Him during our times of lostness and confusion. Where else could we go?)

5. After all the miracles Jesus had performed, after all the teachings He had passed along to them, and after all the time He had spent, Philip suggested that if He could show them God the Father, then the disciples could get along OK. **How did Jesus respond** (vss. 8-11)? (He explained that He was an accurate representation of God the Father. Consequently, they should have already seen plenty.)

6. Based on what you know about Jesus, **what are some things you can tell about God the Father?** (While we may tend to think of God as harsh and angry, we can be assured that He is as patient, compassionate, and loving as Jesus was. Jesus hated pride and stubbornness, but loved humble responsiveness in people.)

7. Jesus made another promise that probably flabbergasted the disciples (vss. 12-14). **What was the last thing you asked for, based on this promise? What was the result? If you could believe this promise a little more, what might you ask for?**

8. Since Jesus would no longer be here with us physically, how did He expect us to carry on (vss. 15-21)? (He promised to send the Holy Spirit to serve as a Counselor when we need help.)

9. Why was it necessary for Jesus to leave? Couldn't He have hung around for a long time and taught us a lot more about God? (His teaching had already been clear and complete. His concern was more for our eternal life than His physical life. His death and resurrection would pave the way for our own. After the Holy Spirit was sent, His disciples would be able to multiply His ministry many times over.)

10. Jesus promised that His people would be able to know He existed even though He wasn't here physically (vs. 19). The rest of the world, however, would not have such insight. What makes the difference (vss. 21-24)? (Love for Jesus results in obedience which in turn leads to a strong relationship between God and believers. Lack of either love or obedience can prevent the growth of that relationship.)

11. This was a traumatic time for Jesus and the disciples. How did Jesus want them to respond to the events that were to come (vss. 25-31)? (With the continued influence of the Holy Spirit, He wanted them to continue to learn, to remember what He had taught them, and to find peace.)

12. Do you think you would have been eager to let Jesus go on while you looked for better things to come, or would you have tried to hold on to Him? Why?

Go back and look at verse 27. Based on this verse, have kids draw pictures of what "peace" means to them, or write a definition of "peace" on the back of the reproducible sheet. Share your drawings/definitions and contrast the peace Jesus gives with anything the world can offer. Then discuss how someone could find peace in the following situations: preparing for a big exam; dealing with a loved one's terminal illness; being nervous about participating in an important sporting event; fearing the possibility of war; and wondering what to do about your future.

Dream Room

Bad news: you have to spend the rest of your life in the same room. Good news: You can design it any way you want (money's no object). Bad news: the room's only so big and you won't be able to fit everything in (like an olympic-size pool). Good news: this is just for pretend. Bad news: but we want you to do it anyway. Good news: Jesus is preparing a room for you that isn't pretend—and it'll be better than anything you can even imagine!

Draw and label what you would put in your "ideal" room. Here are two objects you might be needing to give you an idea of the scale.

BED   TOILET

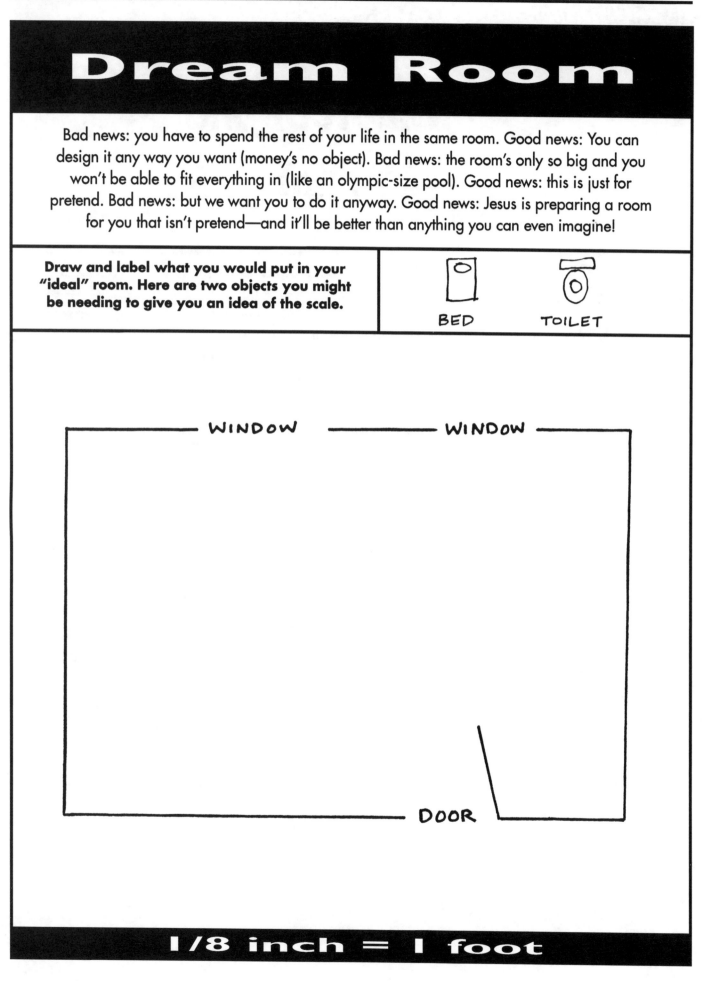

WINDOW — — WINDOW

DOOR

1/8 inch = 1 foot

JOHN 15

The Root and The Fruit

Jesus comforts His disciples as He prepares to leave them. He compares Himself to a vine out of which grow branches—some that are fruitful and others that aren't. And just as some people will hate Jesus, they will also hate His followers. In spite of this, He challenges us to show love for one another, and again promises the coming of the Holy Spirit.

(Needed: Two lipsticks)

Form teams, with one team member behind another in rows. Place a big smear of lipstick on the nose of each team member in the front. At your signal, each team should attempt to pass along the smear by having the second person rub noses with the first, the third with the second, and on down the line. The first team to have lipstick visible on the nose of the last person wins. Compare this passing-along of the lipstick to the branches that grow out of the vine—many people can reflect the characteristics of a single source.

DATE I USED THIS SESSION _____ GROUP I USED IT WITH _____

NOTES FOR NEXT TIME_____

_____

_____

1. Who are some of the people you most respect or admire? In what ways do you try to be like them? Are there some things about them that you don't necessarily wish to imitate?

2. Do you know anyone who is skilled as a gardener? If so, what are some of his or her secrets for growing the best possible plants? (Answers will vary. Focus on the need for pruning.)

3. How did Jesus illustrate our relationship with Him in this chapter, and what point do you think He was trying to make (vss. 1-5)? (He's the vine, we're the branches. Our purpose is to bear "fruit" for the kingdom of God. Fruitless branches are of no use to God, and should be removed. And even the fruitful branches need to be pruned regularly to remain strong and productive.)

4. What can we expect if we try to accomplish good things without being grounded in a solid relationship with God (vss. 4-6)? (We are very limited in the amount of good we can accomplish on our own. Jesus is the One who makes our efforts fruitful.)

5. What is another good reason for remaining solidly attached to the Vine (vss. 7, 8)? (When we are attuned to God's will for us, He provides whatever we need.)

6. Jesus loves us just as much as the Father loves Him (vs. 9). But what do we need to do to experience that degree of love (vss. 9, 10)? (Obey God's commands.)

7. What should be the result of receiving God's love (vs. 11)? (We should experience complete joy in our relationship with God.) **If people observed your level of joy on an average day, how do you think they would rate your obedience level on a scale of 1 (low) to 10 (high)?**

8. What is the proof of real love (vss. 12, 13)? (The willingness to die for someone else.) **How do you think most people would complete this sentence: If you really loved me you'd . . . ?**

9. How had the relationship between Jesus and His followers changed after He willingly gave up His life for them (vss. 14-17)? (They had become His friends as well as His servants.)

10. With all the positive possibilities of being securely attached to the Vine, are there any drawbacks (vss. 18-21)? (Besides the pain of being pruned occasionally, it logically stands that those who oppose Jesus will tend to oppose those who are devoted to Him as well. We can expect a certain amount of hatred and persecution from those people.)

11. Why is it so important for people to respond to what they know to be true about Jesus (vss. 22-25)? (To witness the power of Jesus and know the truth, and then to reject Him, leaves us without excuse. It would be better if we had known nothing at all. A knowledge of Jesus forces us to choose one way or another—His way or our way.)

12. And if we have indeed responded to what we know to be true about Jesus, what else do we need to do (vss. 26, 27)? Who will help us do it? (The Holy Spirit will continue to lead us in the truth, and we should testify to others about what we know.)

Encourage your students to do some inspecting of their own lives in light of the vine and branches analogy presented in this chapter. Hand out copies of the reproducible sheet, "Fruit Inspection," and give group members a few minutes to complete it. Here are some follow-up questions that correspond with the numbered questions on the sheet:

1. What are some specific things you can do to "remain in Jesus"?

2. Give some examples of God's "pruning" activity in your life.

3. What insight does Galatians 5:22-26 add to your answer?

4. How can we strengthen our roots?

5. God wants us to ask Him for opportunities to go and bear fruit. In light of this, what are some things you want to ask of Him?

F·R·U·I·T
I N S P E C T I O N

1 1. Circle the picture that best shows how well attached you are to Jesus, the "Vine."

2 Considering the amount of pruning that needs to be done in your life, which of the following implements should the gardener use?

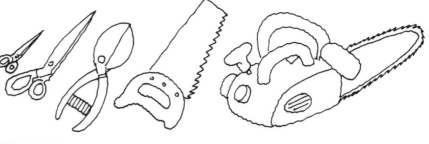

3 Which of the following pictures comes closest to describing the kind of fruit you are bearing in your life?

4 How deep are your "roots" in the faith?

5 In John 15:7, Jesus says, "If you remain in me and my words remain in you, ask whatever you wish, and it will be given you." In the cluster of grapes, write some "words of Jesus" that should be on your mind.

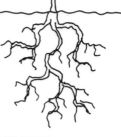

Promises, Promises

As Jesus concludes His challenge to the disciples shortly before His death, He warns them of some of the unpleasant things they can expect because of their association with Him. But He immediately reminds them that the Holy Spirit will be there to see them through any situation. They may have to suffer for a while, but the ultimate result will be joy and peace.

(Needed: Cassette player and tape with different voices on it)

Before meeting, record on a cassette tape a few seconds of ten to twelve different voices (speaking or singing) of people your kids know. Consider recording them off the television, radio, cassettes, or CDs. If you have time, you might even want to slip in some voices from people in your church. Play the tape for your kids and have them write down as many of the voices as they recognize. Award a small prize (optional) to the person who recognizes the most voices. Use this to point out that we need to be listening to the "voice" of the Holy Spirit as we go through our daily routines.

DATE I USED THIS SESSION _____ GROUP I USED IT WITH _____

NOTES FOR NEXT TIME _____

_____

_____

1. If someone wanted to humiliate you publicly, what could he or she do that would really get to you?

2. Jesus tried to warn His followers of hard times and humiliating events that would come after He left. What were some of the things they could expect (vss. 1-4)? (Being put out of the synagogue [which might not sound like much of a punishment, but which was both a religious and social disgrace], and eventually even death.)

3. How could they be expected to cope with such circumstances (vss. 5-11)? (Jesus would send the Holy Spirit to act as counselor for them to know what to do.)

4. What are some of the responsibilities of the Holy Spirit listed in verses 5-11? (Besides being a counselor, He will make clear to a sinful world where they are in error.)

5. In what ways does the Holy Spirit act as our counselor (vss. 12-15)? (Even though Jesus is no longer physically present with us, we can know what He wants us to do through the Holy Spirit. The Spirit helps make God's will known to us, as well as helping us express ourselves before God. [See Romans 8:26, 27.])

6. The disciples were trying to follow everything Jesus was trying to tell them, but they were having a lot of trouble. What was another thing they had trouble understanding (vss. 16-18)? What do you think Jesus was trying to tell them? (Jesus wanted them to know that He was going to die and not be with them physically for "a little while." But later, after His resurrection, they would see Him again.)

7. The disciples were asking each other what Jesus meant, but why do you think they didn't just ask Him? (Most people are reluctant to "show their ignorance." Yet the disciples show us that we could save a lot of needless confusion and anxiety if we were more open to ask for explanations when we need them.)

8. When Jesus did stop to explain, He gave us a great promise: God can turn our grief to joy. What example did

He give to illustrate this truth (vss. 19-22)? (A woman having a baby.) **What others can you think of?** (Being turned down for one job and getting a better one instead; losing a friend or relative, and allowing God's love and peace to fill the void, etc.)

9. **Jesus makes another promise in verses 23 and 24. Do you believe it?** (We can count on God to give us what we need as we go to Him in Jesus' name. Praying "in Jesus' name" involves asking for things that are in accord with His will for us, not simply tacking "in Jesus' name I pray" onto the end of our own wish lists.)

10. **The disciples began to catch on to what Jesus was saying—finally** (vss. 25-30). **But what was the one thing they still weren't entirely prepared for** (vss. 31, 32)? (They would soon be scattered and isolated—away from each other and from Jesus. Yet Jesus assured them that even when they left Him, the Father wouldn't.)

11. **Why was Jesus telling them about all these nasty things that were about to happen** (vs. 33)? (He wanted to prepare them for trouble they would experience in the world without Him, and to assure them that, no matter what, He knew what was going on and they could find peace by trusting Him.)

12. **What are some things that might tend to scare us if we didn't believe God is in control?** (Persecution from nonbelievers; prophecies about the last days, etc. Point out how different our perspective on life is if we truly believe that Jesus has "overcome the world" [vs. 33].)

The reproducible sheet, "This May Hurt a Little," will have your group members examine a number of situations where a little pain is necessary in order to experience a great deal of relief and/or joy. Encourage them to fill in "other" responses. When they finish, discuss: **Why do so many people seem to try to avoid pain altogether these days? What are some things they'll do to avoid pain? Do you think we tend to miss out on a lot of the best things in life if we try to avoid all the painful ones? What can you do to prepare yourself for the next potentially painful experience you will face?**

This May HURT A Little

We all face certain things that don't sound pleasant. Yet some of these things are necessary. For each of the situations listed below, select the most likely response, or fill in a response of your own.

1

You go out for the basketball team, but the coach demands numerous laps and wind sprints before you can even shoot the ball in practice. You go home exhausted every day, and after two weeks you still haven't touched a ball. You think:

___ "I came to play basketball, not to run track. I don't need this. I quit."
___ "I'll simply explain to the coach that he's just asking too much of us."
___ "What a waste of energy! But I guess I'd better do what I'm told."
___ "My, how I enjoy the pain that shoots throughout my body every night, because I know it's making me a much stronger, healthier person."
___ Other:

In the play-offs, you play several grueling games in a row. Some of the players who aren't in such good shape can't keep playing. What are you thinking now?

2

Your older sister is having her first baby. After a few months of morning sickness, feeling her body bloat to the approximate size of Ohio, and wearing clothes that could serve as Boy Scout tents, she's finally ready for the big event. Contractions double her up every five minutes or so, and her calm and ever-efficient husband has whisked her to the hospital (remembering the video camera, of course, and forgetting all her clothes and insurance information.) The delivery room seems full of strangers, all commenting on her disposition. What do you suppose she's thinking?

___ "Oh, wonder. Oh, life. What a blessed miracle! I am filled with joy at the opportunity of bringing a new little one into the world."
___ "It's about time! Let's get this little experience over with!"
___ "Maybe this is all just a bad dream."
___ "I've changed my mind. If my husband wants a baby, let him have it!"
___ Other:

A few hours later as she cradles her tiny son or daughter, what is she thinking?

3

A toothache is just about to kill you. You hurry to the dentist, but when you see the size of the needle, hear the drilling, and smell that . . . whatever it is . . . you think:

___ "On second thought, maybe excruciating pain isn't all that bad."
___ "So what if it's a permanent tooth? A string, a doorknob, a quick push, and this baby's taken care of!"
___ "If I get through this, I'll brush—and floss—30 minutes a night the rest of my life."
___ "I'm very happy to let this person poke, prod, and do whatever he wishes inside my tender mouth, because I know it's for the best."
___ Other:

Fifty years later, when all your friends are losing their teeth, and yours are still in perfect working order, what are you thinking?

JOHN 17

The Prayer of Prayers

With His arrest and death imminent, Jesus spends some time talking to God the Father in prayer. He affirms that He has completed the job His Father sent Him to do—to reveal the plan of eternal life for those who believe in Him. Then He prays for His current disciples and all those who will follow Him throughout the years.

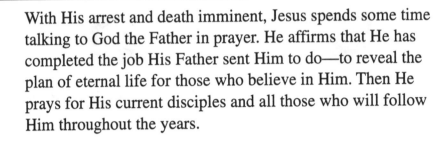

(Needed: Comics pages, scissors)

In advance, cut apart the individual panels of every comic strip on a full page of newspaper comics. Do this as many times as necessary, based on the number of teams you plan to form. During your meeting, form teams and give each team an entire page of cut-apart comics, and see which team can piece them back together the fastest. To be fair, it would be best if each team had an identical set of comics to work with. Our willingness to work together as a team with a united purpose was one of Jesus' concerns in His last prayer before His arrest.

DATE I USED THIS SESSION _____ GROUP I USED IT WITH _____

NOTES FOR NEXT TIME _____

_____

_____

1. When was the last time you said a special prayer before you faced what you knew would be a particularly difficult challenge? What was the tone of the prayer? Did you focus more on yourself, God, or other people?

2. This chapter of John contains Jesus' longest recorded prayer. What was the purpose of this prayer (vss. 1, 2)? (Jesus knew it was time for His arrest and consequential death.)

3. If you knew you would be dying within the next couple of days, how do you think your prayers would sound? What is the tone of Jesus' prayer (vss. 1-5)? (It shows unquestioning respect for God the Father, it is confident, and He seems eager to return to the face-to-face relationship He previously had with His Father.)

4. What did Jesus state as His purpose for coming to earth (vs. 2)? (To bring eternal life to those who believed in Him.) **Based on verse 3, what is eternal life?** (Knowing God the Father and His Son. Note that we can experience eternal life in the present as well as the future.)

5. Jesus spends just a little time focused on Himself and more time praying for His followers. What had been Jesus' goal in working with the disciples (vss. 6-8)? (To give them an accurate picture of God the Father and communicate God's message of love to them. These verses add real significance to Jesus' words in John 16:31 where the disciples believe at last.)

6. What was Jesus' major concern for His disciples at this point (vss. 9-12)? (He prayed for God's protection over them, because He [Jesus] would no longer be there physically to look out for them.)

7. Who do you think Jesus was talking about in verse 12? (Judas.) How do you think He might have felt as this person came to mind?

8. Jesus knew that His followers would still be in the world; yet He prayed that they would not be of the world (vss. 13-16). **What do you think He meant?** (While we are physically present here, we need not buy into "worldly" values and priorities.)

9. **Jesus was certainly sanctified—"set apart for sacred use"** (vss. 17-19). **In what ways are today's believers sanctified?** (Our salvation sets us apart from the rest of the world, but we should also choose to allow God to use us. Our lives should be lived for His glory, not our own.)

10. **Before Jesus concluded His prayer, who else did He pray for** (vs. 20)**?** (Us! [The people who would believe in Him because of the disciples' message.])

11. **What is Jesus' desire for each of us** (vss. 20-23)**?** (To live in complete unity with Himself, God the Father, and each other.)

12. **As Jesus prepared to return to heaven, did He consider His job finished** (vss. 24-26)**?** (His earthly job was almost complete, but He planned to continue to make God known to the people who follow Him.)

The reproducible sheet, "Of the World, or Above the World?" will encourage group members to determine how their own responses to various situations compare to how others might act in those same situations. Ask for volunteers to share their responses. Follow this with a challenge for each person to create something that will remind him or her of the importance of not behaving just like everyone else when things go wrong. You might consider bookmarks or buttons with appropriate slogans: "Not of This World," "I.T.W.B.N.O.T.W" ("In the World, but Not of the World"), "Different Is Cool," or whatever. Without some kind of reminder, it's very easy to stay in the same old (bad) habits.

Of the World, or ABOVE the World ?

In Jesus' famous prayer in John 17, He tells God the Father that His followers are in the world, but not of the world. In other words, we're here with others, but we shouldn't necessarily act like they do. In each of the following situations, share how you think someone who's "in the world and of the world" might respond. Then indicate what your response would be to such an occurrence.

(1) When Joe's girlfriend suddenly dumped him, he felt lousy. She dumped him hard—on his ear. She then went out with someone else that very night and started going steady with the "new guy" the next day. Thoughts of getting even raced through Joe's mind. Everywhere he looked around his room, he saw reminders of her—the teddy bear she gave him for Christmas, her picture on his dresser, two tickets to this Friday's concert on the nightstand. Then, Joe got an idea. He . . .

What would you do if you were in Joe's shoes?

(2) Karen found herself in a hostile argument with her parents over something so insignificant as accidentally leaving the cat in the dishwasher overnight. She was ticked. The icing on the cake, though, was having to explain how she had headed for the library that morning, saying she would have to "study like a maniac" all day, and ended up in the next county with all her friends at the annual Surf and Tan International Beach Party. The more she talked with her parents, the louder their voices became, so she . . .

Of course, if this was you, you'd probably . . .

(3) Kevin and Chip are brothers who happen to share a room together. Statistics warn that there's a slight possibility that people who share a room together might sometimes get on each others' nerves. It seems that 1.3% of the population is composed of finger-drumming, toe-tapping, perpetually humming, deodorant-allergic, food-chomping, color-blind, insect-collecting individuals that have other habits that are a little too annoying to mention. Kevin and Chip both feel the other is one of these people. One day, Kevin found Chip's dirty clothes, school books, cassettes, and butterfly collection on his own side of the room, so he . . .

And your response, if you were Kevin, would be to . . .

JOHN 18

The Beginning Of the End

CHAPTER ✓ CHECK

Having left Jesus and the other disciples earlier, Judas leads a party of soldiers and religious leaders to where they are. Jesus is arrested after a little resistance by the disciples that He squelches. Some of the disciples follow, trying not to be identified. As Jesus is interrogated by the high priest, Peter denies Him three times. Then Jesus is sent on to Pilate, who can't find a basis for the charges against Him.

OPENING ACT

(Needed: A couple of bags of individually wrapped candy)

Have the group sit in a circle and give everyone an equal number of pieces of candy (10 to 20). Each person's goal is to get more by coming up with something that he or she has never done, but that the rest of the group probably *has* done. For instance, the first person might say, "I have never flown on a plane." Everyone who *has* flown on a plane must then give the person a piece of candy. Then the next person in the circle takes a turn. When everyone has had an opportunity to go, have group members take a count of their candy and see who has accumulated the most. Later, you can refer to this as you point out that Jesus is the only person who ever lived who could say, "I have never sinned."

DATE I USED THIS SESSION _____ GROUP I USED IT WITH _____

NOTES FOR NEXT TIME _____

_____

_____

1. Have you ever had any brushes with the law? How does it feel to be stopped by a police officer or some other authority figure? How does it feel to be falsely accused of something?

2. Jesus was not only falsely accused, but He was also betrayed by a close friend. How did He respond to His accusers, and why do you suppose He responded that way (vss. 1-9)? (He knew what was going to happen, so He took the initiative and submitted Himself to them. His demeanor seemed to take them off guard.)

3. How did the disciples respond to this sudden invasion of their privacy (vss. 10, 11)? (Peter appeared to be ready to fight, and inflicted the first casualty, but Jesus quickly stopped him and went with the soldiers willingly.)

4. While Jesus was taken by the Jewish officials (vss. 12-14), the rest of the disciples scattered. But Peter and John ("another disciple," vs. 15) joined the crowd that was following Jesus. Put yourself in Peter's place. For the past three years you've given everything up to follow Jesus. Now He is suddenly arrested, you are something of an accessory, and you have no idea what is going to happen. What would you do the first time someone identified you as an associate of Jesus? What did Peter do (vss. 15-18)? (He lied and denied knowing Jesus, even though it was only a servant girl who questioned him.)

5. Meanwhile, what defense was Jesus using at His trial (vss. 19-21)? (He had done nothing in secret. He suggested the officials question the people who had heard Him speak. [Of course, the Jewish leaders knew Jesus had a lot of public support, so they wanted to convict Him privately.]) What response did Jesus get (vss. 22-24)? (He was mocked and physically abused.)

6. The scene shifts back to Peter, who had had some time to think about what to do. How did he respond the next couple of times he was asked about his connection to Jesus (vss. 25-27)? (Again, he lied and denied knowing Jesus.) Why do you think he continued to deny Him?

7. How do you think Peter felt when the rooster crowed? (See John 13:37, 38. He surely felt miserable because he would have been reminded of Jesus' previous words.)

8. Pilate, the Roman governor, didn't even want to try the case. Why do you think the religious leaders insisted (vss. 28-32)? (They wanted a death sentence. They occasionally held stonings for criminals, but usually the right of execution was reserved by the Romans.)

9. Why do you think Pilate was so interested in what Jesus had to say (vss. 33-37)? (He was a leader, and perhaps he had noticed Jesus' influence over His people. Pilate was also a politician and could probably tell when someone was getting railroaded by a power bloc.)

10. In verse 38, Pilate asks, "What is truth?" How would you answer him? (See John 1:17; 8:32; 14:6; 16:13; and 17:17.)

11. After talking with Jesus, what did Pilate try to do (vss. 38-40)? Why do you think he didn't just do what the religious leaders wanted? (Pilate could find no substantial grounds for condemning Jesus, so he kept trying to convince the insistent leaders to release Him.)

In this chapter, Peter lacked boldness. Later in his life (in the power of the Holy Spirit), Peter demonstrated tremendous courage. The reproducible sheet, "Turning the Tables," will help your group examine another side of boldness—taking the initiative to ask non-Christians questions to get them thinking about Jesus. Go through it together. Pray for opportunities to talk to others about matters of faith, and courage to do so.

Turning the Tables

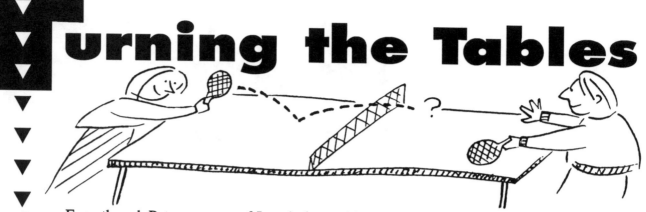

Even though Peter was one of Jesus' closest friends, when the going got rough, he denied Him. You probably won't find yourself in Peter's position very often, but you can show boldness another way—by saying things that get people thinking about God.

Which of the following statements could you see yourself using to get people thinking about spiritual things?

___ Does your family have any kind of spiritual/religious background?
___ Do you think life started by chance, or do you think we were created by Someone?
___ How do you decide if something's right or wrong? What basis do you use?
___ Where are you going? No, I mean when you die!
___ Do you feel happy with your life? How come?
___ Why do you think people believe what they believe?
___ What do you think really matters in life?
___ If you died tonight, where do you think you'd be in the morning?
___ If God asked you why He should let you into heaven, what would you say? (assuming you believed in God, and wanted to go there)
___ What do you feel like you're giving your life to?
___ What do you believe about God?
___ What do you think happens to people after they die?
___ Other _____
___ Other _____

*Notice that all of these are **questions**. Questions call for answers. Asking a question implies that you care enough to listen to the answer. You might be amazed by how many people would actually be interested in talking about some of these questions. They're probably just waiting for someone gutsy enough to ask them, and caring enough to really want to hear what they think.*

Remember: You don't have to play "Gospel dump truck," feeling like you need to explain all the mysteries of the universe in a single conversation. You don't and you couldn't. Share enough to get people thinking and wanting more, but not so much as to bury them.

You don't need a lot of answers to get this process going. Just a few good questions, a couple of good ears, and one big heart.

This Looks Like the End

Jesus, having been sent before Pilate, is mistreated by the Roman soldiers. Yet the more Pilate talks with Jesus, the more he seems to respect Him. The Jewish leaders don't have the power to execute Jesus, and Pilate doesn't have the inclination. But the people are persistent, and fearing for his own future, Pilate finally gives in to their wishes. Jesus is crucified, then buried in the tomb of Joseph of Arimathea.

Have kids write on slips of paper their names and one "secret thing" about themselves that they don't mind revealing. Collect the slips of paper, mix them up, and choose one. Then select two students along with the person whose name is on the slip of paper you chose. Don't let anyone know who the real secret "owner" is. Have the three take seats in front of the group. Read the secret, and then have each one explain the details of the secret (two made-up versions and one real one), trying to convince the group that he/she is the owner of the secret. After all three have talked, have the group vote on who they think is the real secret owner. The one who fools the most people wins that round. Pick another slip and repeat the process. Then discuss the difficult decision Pilate was forced to make in the face of contradictory testimony.

DATE I USED THIS SESSION _____ GROUP I USED IT WITH _____

NOTES FOR NEXT TIME _____

_____

_____

1. What's one of the toughest decisions you ever made? Why was it hard?

2. What things did Jesus have to suffer, even though Pilate found no basis to charge Him (vss. 1-3)? (Flogging; the crown of thorns; mockery [a purple robe and false praise]; and being struck in the face.)

3. As Pilate discussed Jesus' future with the Jewish leaders, they told him something that startled him. Why was Pilate distressed (vss. 4-9)? (He had sensed that Jesus was a decent person, so the Jewish leaders' statement that Jesus claimed to be the Son of God was alarming. What if it were true?)

4. Pilate pressed Jesus on the matter (vss. 10, 11) and wanted to set Him free. You would think that the possibility of Jesus being divine would be enough for Pilate to release Him. But what tactic did the religious leaders use to convince Pilate to do what they wanted (vs. 12)? (They made it a political issue, suggesting that anyone who tolerated Jesus' claim to power could not be true to the Roman Empire.)

5. Pilate finally gave up and ordered Jesus' execution (vss. 13-16). Yet he had one surprise left for the religious leaders who thought they had gotten all they asked for. What did Pilate do, and why do you think he did it (vss. 17-22)? (He had a sign made in three languages stating that Jesus was the King of the Jews. Since the conspirators had forced Pilate to give in, this was Pilate's way of retaliating.)

6. Describe the events of the crucifixion as you think Jesus witnessed them (vss. 18, 23-30). (To His right and left were hanging common criminals; below Him soldiers were gambling for His only possession—His clothes; some of His friends and family members were looking up at Him; He was thirsty and in great pain.) We know Jesus lived without sin. What things might He have been tempted to think, say, or do while on the cross?

7. Why was it significant that Jesus' legs weren't broken, as were the legs of the other two men who were crucified (vss. 31-37)? (The piercing with the spear and the unbroken bones fulfilled two more Old Testament prophecies about Jesus.)

8. Does anything surprise you about the care of Jesus' body after He had died (vss. 38-42)? (It wasn't the disciples, but two community leaders who came forward to take responsibility for Jesus: Joseph of Arimathea and Nicodemus, both of whom had been influenced by the message and life of Jesus.)

9. Of all the people mentioned in this chapter, who best represents where you might have been that day? (Some possibilities: A crucified thief; an accuser; a scared friend hiding in the crowd; or a bold follower of Jesus, standing before Pilate and asking for the body.)

10. How do you feel when reading about Jesus' crucifixion? (Not much, sad, guilty, etc.)

This chapter contains three references to the fulfillment of Old Testament prophecy by Christ's death on the cross (vss. 24, 36, and 37). The reproducible sheet, "Just a Good Guess?" will help your group members see that Jesus had a purpose for visiting this planet, much of which was spelled out in the Old Testament. Have them match the Old Testament prophecies with the New Testament fulfillments. (Answers: 1-K-k; 2-M-l; 3-H-f; 4-B-a; 5-F-d; 6-G-e; 7-D-c; 8-E-b; 9-C-h; 10-I-j; 11-L-m; 12-J-g; 13-A-i.) **What difference does all this make to you, anyway?** (Perhaps seeing all the prophecies and their fulfillments might strengthen one's faith. Maybe some will see connections between the New and Old Testaments that they haven't seen before.)

JUST A GOOD GUESS ?

A lot was written about Jesus before He ever lived on earth. Every prophecy written about Him was fulfilled (three of them in this chapter). Did Jesus read about these prophecies and then go about fulfilling them? Or is there another explanation?

The fact that Jesus fulfilled every one of those prophecies provides a factual pile of evidence on which we must surely come to a conclusion. Below are just a few of the many prophecies concerning Jesus. Draw lines to connect the Old Testament reference (on the left), with the prophecy (center), with the New Testament fulfillment (on the right).

1. Psalm 22:18

2. Psalm 34:20

3. Psalm 78:2, 3

4. Isaiah 7:14

5. Isaiah 9:1, 2

6. Isaiah 53:4

7. Jeremiah 31:15

8. Hosea 11:1

9. Micah 5:2

10. Zechariah 9:9

11. Zechariah 12:10

12. Zechariah 13:7

13. Malachi 3:1

A. Jesus would be preceded by John the Baptist

B. Jesus would be born of a virgin

C. Jesus would be born in Bethlehem

D. Children would be killed in connection with His birth

E. Jesus would be called out of Egypt

F. Jesus would teach in Galilee

G. Jesus would take on our infirmities and sorrows

H. Jesus would teach using parables

I. Jesus would enter Jerusalem on a donkey

J. The disciples would be scattered after Jesus' arrest

K. People would cast lots for Jesus' clothes

L. Jesus' body would be pierced

M. None of Jesus' bones would be broken

a. Matthew 1:20-25

b. Matthew 2:13-15

c. Matthew 2:16-18

d. Matthew 4:12-16

e. Matthew 8:16, 17

f. Matthew 13:34, 35

g. Matthew 26:31

h. Luke 2:4-7

i. Luke 7:24-28

j. John 12:14, 15

k. John 19:23, 24

l. John 19:36

m. John 19:37

Your conclusions:

The End Was Just The Beginning

Upon discovering Jesus' tomb open with no body inside, Mary Magdalene hurries to tell the disciples. As Peter and John check it out for themselves, Mary encounters the risen Christ. Not long afterward, Jesus appears to the disciples. Thomas is not there, and refuses to believe their report. But Jesus returns a week later, when the doubting disciple believes and worships Him.

(Needed: Hard-boiled egg for each person; egg coloring supplies [optional])

Give everyone a hard-boiled egg. If you want, let kids decorate their eggs. Then hold an egg-cracking contest. Pair up and have pairs gently tap their eggs together end-to-end. Eventually, just one of the two should crack. Losers can go ahead and eat their eggs while winners pair up and tap their eggs together again. Continue until just one person is left. Award a small prize if you want. Point out that it's pure fiction that the Easter Bunny brings us eggs. Today's session will help you sort out the facts from the fiction concerning the Easter account.

DATE I USED THIS SESSION _____ GROUP I USED IT WITH _____

NOTES FOR NEXT TIME _____

_____

_____

1. Can you think of a time when you saw or did something that almost put you into shock? (Perhaps an unexpected encounter with a wild animal; a "close call" while driving, etc.)

2. What do you suppose was on Mary's mind as she went to the tomb (vss. 1, 2)?

3. What conclusion had she reached by the time she returned to tell the disciples? (That someone had removed the body. Also notice: Mary says, "we," implying that others were with her.)

4. John was faster, but Peter was more courageous (or at least impulsive). Is there anything important about what Peter saw in the tomb (vss. 3-8)? (If the body was stolen, the grave clothes wouldn't have been left behind and neatly folded.)

5. What effect did this have on the disciples (vss. 8, 9)? (Apparently at least John believed that Jesus had been resurrected, though at this time the only basis for belief was firsthand experience. Only later did the disciples understand it to be a fulfillment of scriptural prophecy.)

6. With nothing else to see, the disciples went back home—but Mary stayed at the tomb. It was certainly worth the wait. First she saw a couple of angels inside the tomb, and then Jesus Himself. She didn't recognize Jesus at first, but how did He make Himself known to her (vss. 10-17)? (He called her by name. John 10:3 adds some deeper meaning to this.)

7. Even today we are unable to fully realize God's presence until we develop a one-on-one relationship with Him. But this is not so hard to do, based on something Jesus told Mary (vs. 17). What was it? (Thanks to Jesus' death and resurrection, God is now our Father as well as His Father.)

8. Considering the disciples' behavior the past few days (deserting, denying, etc.), how might they have felt when Mary told them Jesus was alive again (vs. 18)? How do you think you would have felt about seeing Him?

9. How did Jesus treat the disciples when He first appeared to them (vss. 19-23)? (He was gentle, and His appearance brought them joy. Notice that they were meeting behind locked doors because of fear, but Jesus encouraged them to have peace.)

10. Do you think Thomas showed a lack of faith (vss. 24, 25)? Or do you think he was justified in wanting to see for himself? Defend your answer. (Jesus later gently rebukes Thomas for his reluctance, and we certainly shouldn't expect God to prove everything He says about Himself—just for us—before we are willing to believe. But neither should we be too quick to judge Thomas—at least he eventually came to full belief.)

11. How did Jesus take care of Thomas's doubts (vss. 26-29)? (He offered to let Thomas feel the wounds in His hands and side.) Do you think Thomas actually needed to touch Jesus, or would the offer to do so have been enough for him?

12. What was John's purpose for writing this book (vss. 30, 31)? How well do you think he achieved his purpose? (Review earlier chapters and look for the words "believe," "believed," and "believes.") How would you describe the strength of your belief in Jesus?

A lot of theories have been put forth by those who wish to reject the validity of the resurrection of Jesus Christ. Some of these theories may seem plausible at first, especially if one hasn't accumulated and evaluated the facts surrounding Jesus' death and resurrection. The reproducible sheet, "Fact or Fiction?" helps introduce the group to some of the theories which seek to "explain away" the Resurrection, as well as some historical facts that surround it. Which facts support or contradict each theory?

FACT OR FICTION?

OOPS! WRONG TOMB!

Look over these theories which seek to "explain" the Resurrection as well as some historical facts that surround it. Try to figure out which facts provide "clues" which support or undermine any of these theories.

Theory #1 Jesus didn't die; He just passed out. So He wasn't resurrected at all—He just came to, pushed over the stone, broke through the soldiers, and fled.

Theory #2 The disciples stole Jesus' body while the Roman soldiers slept, then claimed He had been resurrected.

Theory #3 The witnesses who "saw" Jesus after His supposed resurrection had "group" hallucinations. He never really rose again.

Theory #4 The disciples went to the wrong tomb, an empty one, and mistakenly thought Jesus had risen.

Theory #5 The disciples overpowered the Roman soldiers guarding the tomb, took Jesus' body, and then claimed He had been resurrected.

Theory #6 Jesus rose from the dead and proved that God had accepted His sacrifice for sin, and that He is in fact the King of Kings and the Lord of Lords.

FACT: According to John 19:39, the body of Jesus was wrapped tightly in linen cloth with about 75 pounds of spices between the strips of cloth.

FACT: After the body was placed in the tomb, a large stone—possibly weighing up to two tons as was common at that time—was rolled against the entrance of the tomb.

FACT: A Roman guard of strictly trained, intensely disciplined, highly motivated soldiers was stationed in front of the sealed tomb. If a soldier was caught asleep or his post was found unguarded, he was put to death—which encouraged responsibility.

FACT: A Roman seal was placed on the stone at the entrance of the tomb to warn anyone who might try to mess with His body. If anyone broke the seal, that person would be pursued by the Roman army until found and then crucified upside down.

FACT: Both the Romans and the Jewish officials admitted that the tomb where Jesus had been laid was empty (except for the neatly-folded grave clothes)—neither source could deny it.

FACT: The Jewish officials were unable to silence the claims of the disciples—even though all they would have had to do was produce Jesus' body for people to see to totally discredit what the disciples were saying. But they couldn't.

FACT: The same cowardly disciples who deserted Jesus in His hour of need became bold and courageous witnesses about Him virtually overnight, even to the point of being willing to be executed. In fact, according to tradition, all but John were. Would you die for a lie?

FACT: Jesus Christ appeared, alive and well, to over 500 witnesses at one time after His supposed resurrection, not to mention His visiting a whole bunch of different people at different times in different places.

FACT: Even some skeptics of the Resurrection ridicule the idea that Jesus simply passed out, came to, and then escaped. How much inspiration would Jesus, half-beaten-to-death, have instilled in his disciples to cause them to turn the world upside down?

JOHN 21

A Fresh Catch
And a Fresh Start

CHAPTER CHECK

With Jesus no longer around to lead them, Peter decides to go fishing, and many of the other disciples follow him. After catching nothing all night, Jesus (whom they don't recognize) gives them a tip from shore that nets a huge haul. At that point John recognizes Jesus and the disciples hurry to shore. There Jesus fixes them breakfast. He also asks Peter some pointed questions and gives him some instructions.

OPENING ACT

(Needed: Nursery monitor [optional])

After making sure the meeting area is ready, have the leaders disappear. You might go to a separate building, or lock yourselves in a nearby room and remain quiet. If possible, try to monitor what is going on with the group (or have one "accomplice" within the group who can observe and report). See how well your group functions in your absence. How long will kids wait around? Will anyone take the initiative in getting started? After a while, return to the group and discuss how kids felt. Did they feel uncomfortable? Uncared for? Happy to be free from authority? Compare these feelings to the way the disciples must have felt when Jesus was no longer with them.

DATE I USED THIS SESSION _____ GROUP I USED IT WITH _____

NOTES FOR NEXT TIME _____

_____

_____

1. Have you ever failed at something and then gotten a second chance to do better? Describe the situation and how your feelings changed.

2. After Jesus was crucified and no longer with the disciples, it seems that they lacked direction. Peter decided to go fishing (vss. 1-3). **Why do you think he did this?** (That had been his trade before leaving it to follow Jesus. Perhaps he was drifting back to the way life had been before Jesus called him to follow. Maybe he just wanted to keep busy.)

3. Peter and the other disciples who were with him must have been frustrated after fishing all night and not catching anything. **How did they finally manage to succeed** (vss. 4-6)? (Jesus, whom they didn't yet recognize, told them to fish on the other side of the boat.)

4. Why did they suspect that their onshore helper was Jesus? (Besides being a significant feat, the miraculous catch was incredibly similar to one of their earliest encounters with Him. [See Luke 5:1-11.])

5. How did the disciples feel as soon as they recognized that the figure on the beach was Jesus (vss. 7, 8)? (They couldn't get to shore quickly enough. Perhaps after a night out on the sea, away from all the other pressures in their lives, they realized exactly how much they had come to depend upon Jesus. Note Peter's rather odd behavior—he got dressed, then jumped in the water!)

6. How did Jesus react when the disciples landed (vss. 9-14)? (He fixed breakfast for them. Even as their risen Savior, He was a model of servanthood.)

7. But after breakfast, He wanted to attend to a little business that needed taking care of. As Jesus strolled along with Peter, what did they discuss (vss. 15-19)? (Jesus kept asking Peter if he loved Him. And He indicated that such love should be shown by "feed[ing] my sheep.") **What do you think Jesus meant?** (Peter had a bigger job to do than catching fish.) **Why do you think Jesus asked essentially the same question three times in a row?** (Some people suggest that it was to remind Peter of his three previous denials. Jesus was giving Peter a chance to see His grace in the face of Peter's failure. NOTE: It is important that your students understand that the job Jesus gave Peter to do ["feed my sheep"] was to be a *response* of gratitude for Jesus' grace and forgiveness of Him, not as a way to "make up for" his failure.)

8. **What can we learn from Jesus' response when Peter got concerned that he might have to do something different from what John had to do** (vss. 19-23)**?** (Sometimes we have the tendency to get so caught up in whatever other people are doing [or aren't doing] that we lose track of our own responsibilities. We should never lose sight of our own relationship with Jesus by looking around and comparing ourselves to others.)

9. **In concluding his Gospel, John testifies to the accuracy of what he has written. What was one regret he had** (vss. 24, 25)**?** (He just couldn't record everything Jesus did.)

10. **Do you think it would make a difference if we knew a lot more of the things Jesus did? Explain.** (Probably not. More is recorded now than most people will ever be aware of. And the Gospels contain more than enough evidence of Jesus' divine nature for us to believe that He is surely God's Son who came to earth to provide forgiveness for our sins and eternal life.)

SO WHAT?

The reproducible sheet, "Second Chance Theater," will help group members identify with the many characters throughout John's Gospel who were given a second chance. Which one do they most identify with and why? Has everyone in your group taken advantage of the "second chance" Jesus offers him or her?

SECOND CHANCE THEATER

Welcome to Second Chance Theater. Tonight's play was written by that dearly loved playwright, the apostle John. Although written in the first century, its message is just as powerful today. The action revolves around a number of people who met Jesus and how He changed their lives. Sit back and enjoy the show!

Cast *(in order of appearance):*

Nathanael (John 1)—Brother of Philip. Felt nothing good could come out of Nazareth. Eventually became one of the twelve apostles.

Master of the wedding banquet (John 2)—Faced public humiliation when he ran out of wine. Thanks to Jesus, his party became the most famous wedding reception ever.

Nicodemus (John 3)—A Pharisee with a lot of questions. Went to Jesus at night so his peers wouldn't know. A few years later, he helped prepare Jesus' body for burial, undoubtedly ruffling a few of his colleagues' feathers.

Woman at the well (John 4)—A lowly Samaritan with loose morals. After conversing with Jesus, she introduced her whole town to the Messiah.

The official (John 4)—Begged Jesus to heal his son, which He did from a distance. Eventually his whole household believed in Jesus.

Man at the pool (John 5)—Suffered for 38 years, until Jesus healed him. Later, Jesus sought him out and told him to stop sinning. The man went and told the Jewish leaders that Jesus made him well.

Adulterous woman (John 8)—She was guilty under the law and deserved death, but no one was able to cast the first stone. Jesus told her to leave her life of sin.

Blind Man (John 9)—Through no fault of his own, this guy was born blind. Jesus healed him and he boldly worshiped his newfound Lord, despite being thrown out of the synagogue. Causes us to wonder who's really blind anyway.

Lazarus (John 11)—Adds new meaning to the phrase, "second chance." Jesus literally gave him a new life. This caused a big stink among the religious leaders.

Judas (John 13)—Like the others, he had a chance to turn his life around, but he didn't accept what Jesus offered.

Thomas (John 20)—Was full of doubts until Jesus set the record straight.

Peter (John 21)—Even though he denied his Lord three times, Jesus gave him responsibilities and encouraged him to "follow me."

★ ★ **ENCORE:** ★ ★

• Which character do you most identify with? Why?

• What second chances have you been given?